2nd Annual Phillies Minor League Digest

A Fan's View

Steve Potter

Foreword – John Brazer

In 2014 I made my annual trek down to Clearwater, Florida in January to help with the publicity for Phillies Phantasy Camp. There are a lot of perks of having worked for the Phillies organization for the past 24 years, with getting to go to Phantasy Camp right at the top of the list. At Phantasy Camp, you meet many interesting people, from all walks of life, who share an unbridled lifelong passion for the Philadelphia Phillies. However, there was one camper who stood out among the many who eat, drink and breathe all things Phillies... Steve Potter!

Steve is a fixture at the Phillies Minor League Complex once the players start trickling into Clearwater in January to prepare for the upcoming season. I'm the team publicist, but he seemingly has a better relationship with our minor league players, coaches and executives! This past year, Steve was one of the winning bidders in the Phillies annual online auction and was afforded an opportunity to have dinner with team President Andy MacPhail in the Executive Dining Room at Citizen's Bank Park (CBP). During the dinner, Steve was asked by Andy for his assessment of some of the top players in our system. Not only did Steve provide in-depth perspective on the top prospects, but he also included a detailed analysis of guys playing in Single-A or lower. As Steve spoke, you could see that Mr. MacPhail was clearly enjoying the astute observations from a fan who has dedicated his retirement years to his passion for Phillies baseball.

Throughout the year, I am lucky to be included in Steve's regular email blast to Phillies front office executives and announcers providing statistics and detailed insights regarding the young players in our system. In fact, I just received an email from Steve (while typing this foreword) detailing how he would respond as a Phillies executive to the questionnaire that was sent to all 30 Major League Baseball teams from Japanese sensation Shohei Ohtani! I'm also grateful that Steve is a regular guest on my "Baseball Insiders" radio show on WBCB 1490-AM. He provides tremendously valued information about our minor league system in an entertaining fashion. Thanks to Steve, I can ask pertinent questions to Joe Jordan and his staff without feeling like I'm just a "marketing/PR" guy.

As the Phillies continue towards building another World Series caliber team, reading about the minor leaguers in the Second Annual Minor League Digest will shed light on who might be contributors to our team in the future. It's an outlook that will give hope to Phillies fans looking to experience 2008 all over again! As dedicated fans you likely know about players like Kingery, Moniak and Haseley... this book will also arm you with info on budding stars like Sixto

Sanchez, Jhailyn Ortiz and Ranger Suarez. If you make it down to Phillies spring training, look for the Mayor of Carpenter Complex - he'll be there armed with his Phillies Red iPad, taking notes and pictures and a smile on his face!

John Brazer
Director - Publicity
Philadelphia Phillies

Preface:

This is the Second annual digest about the Phillies Minor League system. It's a review of the players in the development stages of their careers, including those taken in the June amateur draft, July international signings and those who played the 2017 season on each of the affiliated teams in the Phillies organization, with projections as to where they progress in 2018.

In this year's digest I've enlisted the help of a few fellow writers and bloggers. While I attempt to watch as many games as possible at each level during the long baseball season, it's not possible for any one person. Helping me out with the digest this go around are the following folks who covered each of the team's they wrote about from a more engaged and on-site day-to-day basis:

Tom Housenick – Sports writer for the *Morning Call* – Tom wrote the summary for the Lehigh Valley IronPigs' season.

Kirsten Karbach – Radio voice of the Clearwater Threshers – Kirsten wrote the summary of the Threshers' season.

Jay Floyd – Writer and Owner of Phoubalz.com – Jay wrote the summary for the Lakewood BlueClaws' season.

Jim Peyton – Lead writer for PhuturePhillies.com – Jim wrote the summary for the Gulf Coast League Phillies.

In addition, photographers Cheryl Pursell, Gail Dull/Baseball Betsy and Mark Wylie are featured with the photos they took during the season. Cheryl contributes photos to the Lehigh

Valley IronPigs and occasionally shoots for the Reading Fightins.

Gail is both a writer and photographer, and her work, along with work from her fellow Phillies blogger husband, known as "Baseball Ross," can be found on BaseballBetsy.com. She focuses primarily on the Clearwater Threshers and the GCL Phillies.

Mark Wylie's photos can be seen regularly on PhuturePhillies.com. The ones featured in this digest are those he took during Fall Instructional League play and also during Gulf Coast League (GCL) play.

Matt Harris edited this year's book. Matt is a freelance writer and content creator whose services are described at mwhcreates.com

Personally, I write about the Phillies and their minor leagues during the season as well. My site is PhilliesBaseballFan.com. We collectively hope that you enjoy our digest of the 2017 Phillies Minor League season and will check out our various sites during the coming seasons as well. I'd like to thank my writing and blogging colleagues for their contributions to this year's book.

Table of Contents:

Chapter One - Spring Training 2017

Spring training for my wife Barb and I is like experiencing Christmas morning every day! We are daily attendees at the Carpenter Complex beginning in mid-January when early arrivals are there working out through the end of March when camp breaks. This season Andres Blanco, Roman Quinn and Odubel Herrera were amongst the first to arrive and we watched their morning workouts, usually 9:00 AM starts. As the days progressed towards the official opening of spring training more and more players arrived, including minor league invitees who were brought in early for injury rehab or specific coaching. Pitchers Kyle Young and Jeff Singer were amongst January arrivals who joined in the pre-camp workouts.

New big league hitting coach Matt Stairs would wave to us each morning as he walked to the cages to watch his young troops hit, many of whom were minor leaguers. I told some of the guys they were indeed privileged to have a major league hitting coach watch and instruct them so early in their careers. New Clearwater Thresher Manager Shawn Williams was a whirlwind of coaching activity, jumping from field to field doing various things like hitting infield, catching bullpens, throwing BP and overseeing outfielder drills. Young coaching assistant Greg Brodzinksi was there every day and was even more active in the various drills than Williams, early on he even participated in batting practice himself and to be honest was one of the more impressive hitters!

Veteran coaches Larry Bowa and Roly de Armas were there most days, the two gents threw BP most every day, something I marveled at as they are both in their 70's. We witnessed the first day Nick Williams came, again an early arrival and the long talk he and coach Bowa had on the third base bench of Roberts field, it was evident that Nick was getting special instruction as other coaches also had what seemed like daily chats with him. I knew he was going to have a big year, I truly believed the pep talks would help him along.

Soon enough in mid-February the official pitchers and catchers reporting day came and players and coaches were in full uniform attire. The fan attendance also picked up as did the autograph seekers. The Phillies initial 40-man roster this year was full of youngsters as the year of transition began, the ascension of multiple talented minor leaguers to the big leagues. Minor League spring camp opened a few weeks afterwards and we watched each home big league game played at Spectrum Field as well as the road games in Dunedin against the Jays (it's only a ten-minute drive from the Phillies Complex). When the big club traveled further away we spent our time watching the minor leaguers play in their daily 1 PM games at the complex, Minor League games are free admission in spring training by the way. We also got to the Complex most mornings to watch the early workouts the guys went through before the games were played.

Camp broke at the end of March and our daily Camp excursions ended for another spring, but we had a full summer of games to look forward to.

Here's some observations made during the Spring Camp.

The big league team finished with a record of 14-17-5, the last time they had a similar record was in 2012 when they went 14-16-4. The 2012 team finished the regular season with an 81-81 record which as camp broke was the stated goal of this year's big league squad.

The team finished spring training with 128 walks which was tops in the Grapefruit League and 5th best overall. The gospel preached to the hitters by coach Matt Stairs was to not give away at bats and to get your pitch to hit, to be "Selfish" in at bats. He also consistently talked about hitting the ball up the middle and not becoming pull happy. Only the Red Sox had more hits this spring in the Grapefruit League than the Phillies 335 (9th overall) and our club was consistently near the middle in most offensive categories.

The starting Pitchers didn't fare well, but the bullpen was relatively solid. The club finished tied for 10th in batting average against at .259 and 7th in WHIP at 1.33. They were 20th in team ERA at 4.82. These numbers were skewed by their 1-6 record against the Yankees including a 14-1 drubbing in the last week of the spring.

Aaron Altherr had a very good spring for the big club. He hit .303 in 66 at bats and led the club in walks with 8. Early in the spring he was striking out a lot, also led the club in that category with 17 but reduced that frequency when he adjusted his swing to be more compact. He hit the longest home run of the spring in Bradenton, a blast that went over the center field batters eye, easily a 430-foot poke!

Freddy Galvis showed that he is one of the best defensive shortstops in baseball, he consistently made all the plays, even the hard ones seemed routine.

Some folks love Odubel, (my wife, my daughter Michelle and I for example) and others not so much. I hoped that the Philly fan-dome wouldn't set too high an expectation because he "got paid" during the offseason as he was rewarded with a multi-year contract. The young man is energetic and talented, to be honest I think the contract he signed was a bargain for the Phillies. Odubel can flat out hit and play, he's going to do things that may drive us fans bonkers but I'd much rather have him on our club than playing against him.

When the Phillies optioned or reassigned the younger kids back to minor league camp the message to each was for them to go back and have a season that forces the brain trust to promote them to the show. It's a challenge that a few ended up delivering upon as 14 players made their major league debut at various times of the 2017 season. (Brock Stassi, Andrew Knapp, Cameron Perkins, Nick Williams, Drew Anderson, Jesen Therrien, Mark Leiter Jr, Ben Lively, Hoby Milner, Ricardo Pinto, Nick Pivetta, Rhys Hoskins, Yacksel Rios and JP Crawford). Stassi and Knapp made the club out of spring training with Stassi being the ultimate "hard work pays off" story. He made the show after being a 33rd round draft selection in the 2011 draft beating very long odds to do so.

First baseman Darick Hall had a tremendous Minor League camp, he seemingly was always on base and hit every ball on the screws. It was an easy prediction that he was going to have a big year. Young pitcher Sixto Sanchez sparkled and showed why scouts rave about his future.

The minor league camp awards were as follows:

Larry Rojas Award: Sixto Sanchez

The award is given annually to the best international player in minor league camp.

Bill Giles Award – Cole Stobbe

The award is given annually to the best American born player in minor league camp.

John Vukovich Award – Doug Mansolino

The award is given annually to the coach who exemplifies the spirit and dedication that Coach Vukovich displayed during his coaching tenure.

Chapter Two - Season Recap – Lehigh Valley IronPigs

Tom Housenick of the Morning Call wrote the following recap of the 2017 Lehigh Valley season. He's the beat writer for the club for the Morning Call newspaper.

Lehigh Valley's 10th year of existence was a tale of two seasons. IronPigs fans relished much of the first half because manager Dusty Wathan's club was among the best record-wise at any level of Minor League Baseball.
The second half, which began on June 30, was the one Phillies fans hope will lead the major-league team back to respectability and, eventually, playoff caliber.

Lehigh Valley made the International League playoffs for the second year in a row despite spending the last two-plus months plugging holes left by the Phillies who plucked many of the organization's top prospects.

It started on June 30, when outfielder Nick Williams received his first major-league promotion. It lasted through the end of the regular season because Williams, one of the most athletically gifted prospects in any organization, had an .811 OPS with 55 RBIs in 83 games with the Phillies. A year after letting his emotions get the best of him in his desire to reach the majors, Williams showed that he possesses all the skills necessary to make him a significant piece of Philadelphia's future.

Rhys Hoskins, Jorge Alfaro, J.P. Crawford and several pitchers followed Williams' path down the Northeast Extension of the Pennsylvania Turnpike throughout the summer.
Hoskins' historic power surge was well documented and showed why he is a cornerstone for the next decade at first base. Alfaro was supposed to spend all of 2017 in Triple-A,

but an injury to Andrew Knapp allowed the talented but inconsistent catcher to spend the last two months with the Phillies. He batted .318, but his lack of discipline at and behind the plate showed that he is not yet a finished product.

Crawford was called up minutes after the IronPigs won their sixth consecutive game to end the regular season and clinched a wild-card berth. Playing his natural shortstop position as well as third base, Crawford, the organization's top-ranked prospect at the start of three consecutive seasons, provided flashes of what he can be in the field and at the plate.

Lehigh Valley lost six of its first nine games in 2017, which projected to be its best season in history.
Many of the IronPigs' top players were prospects getting their first taste of Triple-A, so there figured to be an adjustment period for them. With Wathan in his initial season as a Triple-A manager after spending the previous five at Double-A Reading, Lehigh Valley quickly regrouped to win nine of its next 12.

The month of May proved to be what everyone was hoping. After splitting the first four games of the month, the IronPigs won a franchise-record 12 games in a row and finished the month winning 24 of 29 games and owned the minors' best record in the first week of June.
Williams, Hoskins, Alfaro and Crawford were there for the record-setting stretch. Outfielder Dylan Cozens, who possesses the organization's most power potential, struggled for much of 2017, and likely will start 2018 back in Lehigh

Valley. He did provide a highlight few at Coca-Cola Park will forget when he hit a 469-foot home run out the park in right-center field. Cozens set other Lehigh Valley record for games played and strikeouts.

Not all the Phillies' top prospects started the year with the IronPigs. Starting pitcher Tom Eshelman made his Triple-A debut with eight shutout innings of a May 8 win over visiting Rochester. Four starts later, he had just the third 9-inning, complete-game shutout in IronPigs history with his 112-pitch gem in Indianapolis. Eshelman later started the Triple-A All-Star Game, was named the IronPigs pitcher of the year as well as a Paul Owens Award winner as the Phillies minor-league pitcher of the year.

Hoskins was the International League's MVP and rookie of the year, despite not playing in the minors after Aug. 9. He led the IL in six offensive categories at the time of his promotion: home runs, RBIs, slugging percentage, runs scored, OPS and walks.

Another prospect, second baseman Scott Kingery, arrived with a bang on June 26. He made a leaping, backhand catch of a liner destined for center field in the first inning of his first Triple-A game. Kingery hit .291 with 41 runs and a franchise-record 23-game hitting streak in 63 Triple-A games. His defense and base running remained stellar, too. Phillies fans should see him in Philadelphia in mid-May, 2018.
Several other pitching prospects made their way to Lehigh Valley, including Brandon Leibrandt, son of former major leaguer Charlie Leibrandt; Jose Taveras, Drew Anderson and Yacksel Rios.

Other, more familiar, names spent less than a full season with the IronPigs for a variety of reasons. Ben Lively earned multiple promotions to the Phillies. Jake Thompson also spent his share of time in Philly, though his struggles in Lehigh Valley led to him setting a team record for losses (14). The right-hander did pitch to a 2.73 ERA with opponents hitting .230 in his five September starts for the parent club.

Nick Pivetta made only five Triple-A starts because he was needed by the Phillies. Zach Eflin's elbow issues were part of why he pitched just eight times for the IronPigs.
Pedro Beato, a 31-year-old who previously pitched in the Orioles, Mets, Red Sox and Braves organizations, set a Lehigh Valley record with 33 saves in 35 chances. His save total is a Phillies' Triple-A record and the most in the International League since 2010. He also was a Triple-A midseason and postseason All-Star thanks to a 2.75 ERA and a 1.096 WHIP in 52 appearances.

Lehigh Valley finished the regular season with an 80-62 record, which was tied with Rochester for second place in the International League North Division. The IronPigs claimed the wild card thanks to winning the season series from the Red Wings.

Wathan's club lost their first-round postseason series to rival and IL North Division champion Scranton/Wilkes-Barre in four games of a best-of-five.

Here's a look at the Lehigh Valley "numbers" for 2017.

Win - Loss Record 80 - 62

2nd - International League Eastern Division (6 team Division)

Winner of the Wild Card Playoff Spot

Lost in First Round of Playoffs to Scranton 3 games to 1

Team Statistics: 14 team League

Hitting:

At Bats - 11th - 4,658
Runs - 6th - 624
Hits - 11th - 1,158
Doubles - 12th - 217
Triples - 4th - 31
Home Runs - 2nd - 152
RBIs - 5th - 585
Total Bases - 6th - 189
Walks - 6th - 449
Least Strikeouts - 12th - 1,242
Stolen Bases - 10th - 64
OBP - Tied for 9th - .320
Slugging Pct. - 3rd - .406
Batting Average - 13th - .249
OPS - 4th - .727

Pitching:

ERA - 6th - 3.72
Complete Games - Tied for 2nd - 5
Shutouts - 3rd - 15
Saves - 1st - 44
IP - 11th - 1,224
Least Hits Allowed - 5th - 1,167
Least Runs Allowed - 7th - 578
Least Earned Runs Allowed - 6th - 506
Least Home Runs Allowed - 7th - 111
Least Hit Batters - 2nd - 36
Least Walks - 3rd - 410
Most Strikeouts - 12th - 1,022
Holds - Tied for 4th - 46
WHIP - 5th - 1.29

Individual League Leaders - Hitting - (Top 10 in League):

Games - Dylan Cozens - 3rd - 136 (Lehigh Valley Franchise Record)
At Bats - Dylan Cozens - 10th - 476
Runs - Rhys Hoskins - 2nd - 78, JP Crawford - Tied for 3rd - 75, Dylan Cozens - Tied for 8th - 68
Triples - JP Crawford - Tied for 2nd - 6
Home Runs - Rhys Hoskins - 3rd - 29, Dylan Cozens - 4th - 27
RBIs - Rhys Hoskins - 1st - 91, Dylan Cozens - 5th - 75
Total Bases - Rhys Hoskins - 3rd - 233
Walks - JP Crawford - 1st - 79, Rhys Hoskins - 6th - 64, Dylan Cozens - 10th - 58
Strikeouts - Dylan Cozens - 1st - 194
OBP - Rhys Hoskins - 2nd - .385
Slugging Percentage - Rhys Hoskins - 1st - .58

Batting Average - Rhys Hoskins - 8th - .284
OPS - Rhys Hoskins - 1st - .966

Individual League Leaders - Pitching - (Top 10 in League):

Wins - Tom Eshelman - Tied for 5th - 10
Losses - Jake Thompson - Tied for 1st - 14
ERA (minimum 0.8 IP/league game) - Tom Eshelman - 2nd - 2.23
Games - Pedro Beato & Pat Venditte - Tied for 3rd - 52, Michael Mariot - 8th - 45
Starts - Jake Thompson - Tied for 4th - 22
Complete Games - Tom Eshelman - 2nd - 3
Shutouts - Tom Eshelman - Tied for 3rd - 1
Saves - Pedro Beato - 1st - 33
WHIP (minimum 0.8 IP/league game) - Tom Eshelman - 1st - 0.94
Holds - Michael Mariot - Tied for 3rd - 9
Games Finished - Pedro Beato - 1st - 48

Tom Eshelman – Photo by Cheryl Pursell

Rhys Hoskins – Photo by Cheryl Pursell

Dylan Cozens – Photo by Cheryl Pursell

Jorge Alfaro – Photo by Cheryl Pursell

JP Crawford – Photo by Cheryl Pursell

Logan Moore – Photo by Cheryl Pursell

Ben Lively – Photo by Cheryl Pursell

Jose Taveras – Photo by Cheryl Pursell

Nick Williams – Photo by Cheryl Pursell

JP Crawford & Scott Kingery – Photo by Cheryl Pursell

Cam Perkins & Brock Stassi – Photo by Cheryl Pursell

Chapter Three: Season Recap – Reading Fightin's

Gregg Legg managed the club this year in his second stint at Reading, as he was the skipper also from 2002-04. Legg has been with the Phillies organization for 36 years, serving in various minor league capacities after being drafted as a player in 1982 and working his way to the major leagues in 1986 as a middle infielder. For the past two summers he managed at Clearwater.

He was assisted by pitching coach Steve Schrenk who spent his second-straight year at Reading, where he was also pitching coach in 2009 for the club. Schrenk has been a pitching coach in the Phillies organization since 2004 after finishing up a 16-year pro career as a pitcher, including two years with the Phillies. The hitting coach was John Mizerock, his first season at Reading but sixth with the organization. He split last season between Williamsport and Lehigh Valley after being on the Major League staff in 2015 as the catching/assistant hitting instructor. Greg Brodzinski completed his first full season as an assistant coach. The 26-year-old was the 18th round draft choice of the Phillies in the 2015 draft. Mickey Kozack was the team's trainer, his first stint at Reading but 11th with the Phillies, for the prior three seasons he served as the trainer for the Clearwater Threshers.

It was a young team, with the average age of 23.54 years old among the 25 active players listed on the roster at the end of July, when I did a league-wide age analysis. Going deeper into the analysis showed the average age of the pitchers coming in at 23.38 years old and the position players average age of 23.23 years. In comparison, the league average age at the same time showed the league average at 24.53 (Pitchers 24.67 years, and Position Players 24.39 years.) Reading was the youngest team overall in the league and had the youngest pitching staff as well. The team employed 30 different position players this summer and 32 Pitchers.

Here's a look at the "numbers" for 2017.

Win - Loss Record 72 - 68

3rd Place - Eastern League Eastern Division (6 team Division)

Team Statistics: 12 team League

Hitting:

At Bats - 2nd - 4,700
Runs - 3rd - 642
Hits - 2nd - 1,226
Doubles - 2nd - 240
Triples - 5th - 30
Home Runs - 1st - 153
RBIs - 3rd - 590
Total Bases - 2nd - 1,985
Walks - 10th - 423
Least Strikeouts - 9th - 1,080
Stolen Bases - 5th - 87
OBP - 10th - .326
Slugging Pct. - 2nd - .422
Batting Average - Tied for 3rd -.261

Pitching:

ERA - 4th - 3.94
Saves - 9th - 35
IP - 3rd - 1,214
Least Hits Allowed - 3rd - 1,157
Least Runs Allowed - 4th - 600
Least Earned Runs Allowed - 4th - 532
Least Home Runs Allowed - 11th - 134
Least Walks - 8th - 467
Most Strikeouts - 10th - 960
WHIP - 3rd - 1.34
Holds - 3rd - 32

Individual League Leaders - Hitting - (Top 10 in League):

Runs - Jiandido Tromp - 9th - 64
Hits - Carlos Tocci - 7th - 132, Jiandido Tromp - 8th - 130
Doubles - Jiandido Tromp - 2nd - 31
Triples - Carlos Tocci - Tied for 1st - 7, Scott Kingery - Tied for 2nd - 5, Mitch Walding - Tied for 3rd - 4
Home Runs - Mitch Walding - 4th - 25, Kyle Martin - Tied for 7th - 22, Scott Kingery & Jiandido Tromp - Tied for 9th - 18
RBIs - Kyle Martin - Tied for 10th - 68
Total Bases - Jiandido Tromp - 4th - 221
Strikeouts - Kyle Martin - Tied for 3rd - 134, Mitch Walding - 5th – 127

Stolen Bases - Zach Coppola - 2nd - 29, Scott Kingery - 7th - 19

OBP - Carlos Tocci - 10th -.362

Slugging Percentage - Mitch Walding 4th - .516, Jiandido Tromp - 8th - .485

Batting Average - Carlos Tocci - Tied for 2nd - .307

OPS - Mitch Walding - 6th - .842

Individual League Leaders - Pitching - (Top 10 in League):

Wins - Tyler Viza - Tied for 4th - 10, Drew Anderson - Tied for 5th - 9

Starts - Tyler Viza - Tied for 2nd - 26

Saves - Victor Arano - Tied for 9th - 9

IP - Tyler Viza - Tied for 8th - 139.2

Holds - Austin Davis - Tied for 4th - 9

Games Finished - Victor Arano - Tied for 8th - 24

Beyond the Numbers:

Like every club in the Phillies organization this summer there was a great deal of player transition. Scott Kingery and Andrew Pullin were both having monster years at Reading which earned them June promotions to Lehigh Valley. Kingery hit .313/.379/.608 in 69 games (278 at bats) with 18 home runs and 19 stolen bases. Pullin hit .308/.368/.556 in 67 games (266 at bats) with 14 home runs and 22 doubles. Carlos Tocci (.307/.362/.398 in 113 games (430 at bats) also stood out and earned a later promotion to the Triple-A level as well. They were replaced by the subsequent promotions of Drew Stankiewicz, Damek Tomscha and Cord Sandberg coming up from Clearwater after having successful years there.

Mitch Walding had a breakout power year hitting 25 home runs despite slashing a .236/.327/.536 line in 351 at bats. He also missed a month of the season after suffering a broken nose on an infield collision with catcher Chace Numata. Walding was promoted to Lehigh Valley for their playoff series with Scranton/Wilkes-Barre. The 25-year-old has always been a slick fielder at third base, and he'll get a shot next spring to be the regular third baseman for Lehigh Valley in 2018.

23-year-old outfielder Jiandido Tromp quietly had a very nice season. He slashed .285/.329/.485 in 456 at bats at the AA level with 18 homers and 62 RBIs.

Damek Tomscha (26 years old) put together a very good season hitting .307/.386/.439 combined between Clearwater and Reading in 374 at bats. He played first base, third base and left field this summer and finished with a batting average over .300 at both levels played this year. He's a career .282 hitter.

Zach Coppola, 23 years old, also had a nice summer. He hit a combined .285/.357/.328 in 485 at bats between Clearwater and Reading and stole 39 bases. He's a Richie Ashburn prototype as a leadoff hitter.

The pitching staff also was one of transition as opening day roster guys like Tom Eshelman, Brandon Liebrandt, Alexis Rivero, Yacksel Rios and Jesen Therrien all were promoted in the first half of the year or shortly after the All-Star break. Rios posted a 0.84 WHIP and a 1.89 ERA in 38 IP and

Therrien had a 0.59 WHIP and 1.26 ERA in 28.2 IP as they were dominant relievers while at Reading. Cole Irvin, Franklyn Kilome, Austin Davis, Jeff Singer, Jacob Waguespack and Garrett Cleavinger replaced them, up from Clearwater. All could work their way further up the ranks yet again in 2018.

Scott Kingery – Photo by Cheryl Pursell

Carlos Tocci – Photo by Cheryl Pursell

Andrew Pullin – Photo by Cheryl Pursel

Yacksel Rios – Photo by Cheryl Pursell

Jiandido Tromp – Photo by Cheryl Pursell

Mitch Walding – Photo by Cheryl Pursell

Drew Anderson – Photo by Cheryl Pursell

Drew Stankiewicz – Photo by Cheryl Pursell

Chapter Four: Season Recap – Clearwater Threshers

Kirsten Karbach wrote the following recap of the 2017 Thresher season. She's the radio voice of the Threshers who just completed her fifth year as the play-by-play broadcaster for the club.

Harold Arauz had thrown just 63 pitches in six perfect innings on a rainy Sunday afternoon. Game two of a doubleheader on July 30 saw the Threshers' 22-year-old righty make quick work of the Fort Myers Miracle. Arauz flipped in curveballs and upper-80s fastballs. He whiffed five in a row at one point, and not a single ball left the infield before Jaylin Davis flew out to open the sixth inning. A walk to Brandon Lopez broke up the perfect game with one out in the seventh, but the Panama-native was untouchable, setting a career-high with 10 strikeouts while spinning a seven-inning no-hitter.

Pitching was the theme of the 2017 season for the Phillies' Advanced-A affiliate, with Arauz's no-no topping the list of dominant outings spun by Clearwater's talented arms. While the Threshers lacked the impact bats of years past, fans at Spectrum Field witnessed the most prolific and impactful pitching talent to come through Clearwater in the last five years.

With manager Shawn Williams at the helm, the Threshers stayed competitive down to the wire in both halves, falling one game short of clinching the Florida State League North in the first half, and battling through a tough month of August that saw the Dunedin Blue Jays clinch the second playoff spot in the final series of the regular season. Overall, Clearwater finished 67-71, third place in the FSL North.

The Threshers rotation weathered a near-complete turnover from Opening Day to season's end, but of the eight hurlers who made at least 10 starts, seven of them posted ERAs of 3.00 or less.

The 2017 Opening Day rotation featured the likes of Jose Taveras, Cole Irvin, Franklyn Kilome, Alberto Tirado, Blake Quinn, and Seranthony Dominguez, as Clearwater featured a six-man rotation for the second-straight year.

Yet it was right-hander Zach Eflin who toed the rubber in the season opener, making a rehab appearance after a pair of knee surgeries. Eflin twirled five innings of one-hit ball before handing a 3-0 lead over to Dominguez in his Threshers debut. The right-hander made a quick impression, flashing an upper 90s fastball mixed with an effective slider.

Dominguez's first start of the season on April 12 at Lakeland was electric. He cruised through the first inning, reaching 99 MPH on the Publix Field radar gun on his way to striking out the side. He mowed down the first two he faced in the second inning, and struck out seven of the first eight batters of the game in three perfect innings. Dominguez ultimately allowed one run on three hits and struck out 10 batters in six innings to earn the win. Unranked by both Baseball America and MLB.com entering the season, Dominguez was on his way to a breakout year before a shoulder issue forced his early exit in the fifth inning against the Tampa Yankees on May 13. He returned two months later and showed flashes of his early-season brilliance while working to regain his command after the lengthy layoff.

Dominguez's fastball easily sits 96-97 MPH. He controlled his upper-80s slider well before the injury, showed an occasional curve, and worked on developing his high-80s changeup throughout the season.

Ranked by Baseball America as the No. 7 prospect in the Phillies system entering 2017, Kilome also fires home a mid-90s fastball, and the right-hander turned in a strong season in Clearwater. In 19 starts, Kilome posted a 2.59 ERA before moving up to Double-A Reading on August 5.

While not possessing the same high-octane velocity, Taveras and Irvin were the most polished hurlers to take the hill for Clearwater in 2017.

Taveras earned the starting nod in the Florida State League All-Star Game, and soared all the way to Triple-A Lehigh Valley by the month of August. The right-hander's fastball worked in the upper 80s to low 90s, but Taveras keeps hitters off balance with one of the better changeups in the organization.

Irvin, a fifth round draft pick out of the University of Oregon in 2016, walked only 14 batters in 67 innings as a Thresher, posting a 2.55 ERA before his late-June promotion to Double-A Reading. A student of the game, the southpaw varies his fastball, adding and subtracting with a two-seam, four-seam, and one-seam. Irvin works quickly, commands his changeup, and mixes in both a slider and curveball.

The month of May saw Quinn and Tirado flip to the bullpen, while Edgar Garcia and Jacob Waguespack each earned their first extended opportunities to develop in a starting role.

Garcia's slider was rated by Baseball America entering 2017 as the best in the Phillies farm system. The 20-year-old, who had made seven career starts prior to joining the Clearwater rotation on May 20, posted a 4.11 ERA as a starter and 4.47 overall as the youngest hurler on the Opening Day roster.

Waguespack is arguably the most underrated arm in the Phillies farm system. The 6'6" right-hander went undrafted out of Ole Miss, but signed with the Phillies after his junior year in 2015. He has revamped his entire repertoire since then, adding more than five MPH in fastball velocity and implementing a hard cutter that profiles as a big-league pitch. His curveball and changeup, which he seldom used out of the bullpen, both showed notable improvements since joining the rotation.

Waguespack had served exclusively as a reliever in his career prior to May 25, when he held the Florida Fire Frogs to just a run on three hits in what was then a career-most five innings of work. He yielded two runs or less in each of his first seven starts, and was promoted to Reading on July 31. Waguespack put a bow on a breakout season with an impressive six innings of one-run ball for the Triple-A Lehigh Valley IronPigs in the International League playoffs.

Riding the strength of its pitching, Clearwater finished 16-8 in April and led the FSL North for the majority of the first half, before the Tampa Yankees managed to pull even in the race heading into the All-Star break.

After six Threshers All-Stars helped the North division to a 5-2 win in the 56th FSL All-Star Game, Clearwater entered the final three games of the first half needing only to match

Tampa, as the Threshers owned the tiebreaker over the Yankees.

Clearwater took two of three from the Bradenton Marauders, one of the tougher teams in the FSL South, but came up short of a playoff berth as the Yankees swept the struggling Florida Fire Frogs to clinch the First Half title.

With a new-look rotation, pitching was again the intrigue of the second half. While the more experienced arms of Taveras and Irvin progressed to the higher levels of the Phillies system, Clearwater's rotation received the young, highly touted hurlers JoJo Romero, Ranger Suarez and, later, Philadelphia's top pitching prospect Sixto Sanchez, all promoted from Lakewood.

Romero transitioned to Clearwater with ease, whiffing 19 batters over his first two starts while permitting only an unearned run. At 20 years old, Romero surrendered more than three runs in a start just twice all season, with a 2.16 ERA combined between Clearwater and Class-A Lakewood. The southpaw possesses an expansive repertoire, with a four-seam fastball, sinker, and newly developed cutter, a changeup, a slider and a curveball.

Suarez came to Clearwater in July after putting up a sparkling 1.59 ERA in Class-A Lakewood. The lefty, who turned 22 in August, did not allow a run in his first two starts as a Thresher. Despite a couple of tough outings at the end of the year, he posted an ERA of 3.82 and struck out a batter per inning in his eight starts.

Sanchez is the top-rated arm in the Phillies' farm system, and the reason is clear. His fastball frequently hits triple-digits, easily sitting at 97 MPH. Sanchez, who turned 19 on July 29, is a quick worker, and he pounds the strike zone. While still developing as a pitcher - Sanchez was previously an infielder and did not pitch until he signed - his raw ability is without question.

Despite the abundance of talent on the mound, slowly but surely the bats that carried the Clearwater order early in the season earned promotions up to Reading. Speedy outfielder Zach Coppola was the first, after batting .392 in a scorching month of May. Drew Stankiewicz emerged as a Florida State League All-Star and hit .263 as the Threshers everyday second baseman, earning the move up to Double-A on June 22. The ever-consistent Damek Tomscha hit .303 for the Threshers before a stint on the disabled list and a subsequent jump to Reading on July 13.

Clearwater stayed in the race until the final series, despite a nine-game skid from August 7-15 that opened when a seven-run lead slipped away in a 13-11 loss at Tampa. The Threshers went just 8-19 in the month of August.

The most highly-touted bat to come through Clearwater in 2017 was former first round pick Cornelius Randolph, and while the numbers won't jump off the page, Randolph made perhaps the biggest strides offensively for any Thresher throughout the summer.

Randolph was just 19 years old when the season began, and had been limited to 63 games in Lakewood due to injury in 2016. He hit .203 in April, but batted 30 points higher in each successive month until cooling down in August, ultimately settling at .250 on the season. Randolph, who had homered just three times total though his first two professional seasons, showed tremendous progress in the power department by knocking 13 home runs, which ranked eighth in the league. His 55 walks drawn were a team-high, and seventh-most in the FSL.

Center fielder Mark Laird put himself in the running for a minor league Gold Glove after turning in the only errorless season by a Florida State League outfielder in the last five years. Like Randolph, Laird showed immense progress in reworking his approach. An opposite-field hitter in college at LSU, Laird made noticeable strides in becoming an all-fields threat, stinging the ball to the pull side with improving frequency. He ultimately hit .286, finishing sixth in the league.

While Laird shined defensively in center, Clearwater also benefited from superb defense behind the plate. Deivi Grullon gunned down 36.9 percent of baserunners in his 71 games in Clearwater. Edgar Cabral, who joined the Threshers on July 27, threw out 13-of-24 would-be base-stealers, an impressive 54.2 percent. Austin Bossart also nabbed 44.9 percent of potential base stealers while posting the lowest catcher's ERA on the team (2.95) for the second-straight year.

Not to be overlooked, lefty Austin Davis emerged as a top bullpen arm early, posting a 2.01 ERA and walking just three batters across 10 outings to earn an early May promotion to Double-A. Deadline acquisition JD Hammer flashed a mid-90s fastball and improved with each subsequent outing, dominating to the tune of a 0.57 ERA in 12 games after a trade from the Rockies system as part of the Pat Neshek deal. Southpaw Jeff Singer and right-hander Seth McGarry tied for the league-lead with 19 saves, and Trevor Bettencourt held opponents to a .157 average and put up a 1.57 ERA in 16 games after a midseason promotion from Lakewood.

The Threshers pitching staff set a Clearwater record with 1,191 strikeouts in 2017, surpassing the previous mark of 1,161 set in 2012. It was Bettencourt who notched the record-breaking K, cutting down the Blue Jays' Cavan Biggio looking in the eighth inning on August 31.

Philadelphia began to see an influx of big bats in 2017, with the likes of Rhys Hoskins, Nick Williams, and JP Crawford, and all-around threat Scott Kingery poised to make his mark in the very near-future. The biggest hole in the Phillies system - which was ranked sixth-best by Baseball America entering the year - has been a lack of frontline starting pitching.

From the power arms of Sanchez and Dominguez, to the finesse of Irvin and Taveras, to the underrated talent of Waguespack and the versatile threat Romero - rest assured. Those impact arms are busy rising through the Philadelphia farm system.

Here's a look at the "numbers" for 2017.

Win - Loss Record 67-71 overall (38-32 1st Half, 29-39 2nd Half) (38-34 Home, 29-37 Away)

3rd Place Overall - Florida State League North Division (6 team Division)

2nd Place - First Half and 4th Place - Second Half

Team Statistics: 12 team League

Hitting:

At Bats - 3rd - 4,571
Runs - 10th - 494
Hits - 2nd - 1,151
Doubles - 7th - 199
Triples - 9th - 26
Home Runs - 1st - 104
RBIs - 9th - 453
Total Bases - 2nd - 1,722
Walks - 10th - 354
Least Strikeouts - 6th - 1,083
Stolen Bases - 9th - 86
OBP - 9th - .313
Slugging Pct. - 3rd - .377
Batting Average - 5th - .254
OPS - 6th - .690

Pitching:

ERA - 4th - 3.16
Shutouts - 4th - 14
Saves - 2nd - 40
IP - 4th - 1,199.1
Least Hits Allowed - 6th - 1,094
Least Runs Allowed - 4th - 494
Least Earned Runs Allowed - 4th - 421
Least Home Runs Allowed - 12th - 95
Least Walks Allowed - 6th - 405
Most Strikeouts - 2nd - 1,191
WHIP - 5th - 1.25, Holds – 8th – 32

Individual Batting League Leaders (Top 10 in League):

Games - Cornelius Randolph - Tied for 6th - 122, Wilson
Garcia - Tied for 7th - 121
At Bats - Wilson Garcia - 4th - 477
Hits - Wilson Garcia - Tied for 2nd - 131
Doubles - Wilson Garcia - 4th - 28
Triples - Cornelius Randolph - Tied for 5th - 5
Home Runs - Jan Hernandez - Tied for 2nd - 16, Cornelius
Randolph & Wilson Garcia - Tied for 5th - 13
RBIs - Wilson Garcia - Tied for 5th - 60, Cornelius Randolph -
Tied for 8th - 58
Total Bases - Wilson Garcia - 1st - 202, Cornelius Randolph -
7th - 177
Walks - Cornelius Randolph - 6th - 55
Strikeouts - Jose Pujols - 2nd - 150, Cornelius Randolph - 8th -
125

Slugging Percentage - Wilson Garcia - 6th - .423

Individual Pitching League Leaders (Top 10 in League):

Games - Seth McGarry - Tied for 1st - 44 (31 with Bradenton, 13 Clearwater), Luke Leftwich - Tied for 3rd - 42, Jeff Singer - Tied for 8th - 37, Tyler Gilbert - Tied for 10th - 35
Shutouts - Harold Arauz - Tied for 1st - 1
Saves - Jeff Singer & Seth McGarry - Tied for 1st - 19 (McGarry had 14 with Bradenton, 5 with Clearwater), Luke Leftwich - Tied for 5th - 8
Holds - Tyler Gilbert - Tied for 2nd - 6

Games Finished - Seth McGarry - 1st - 38, Jeff Singer - 2nd - 33, Luke Leftwich - Tied for 6th - 20, Tyler Gilbert - Tied for 9th - 15

Jo Jo Romero – photo taken by Gail Dull/Baseball Betsy

Jacob Waguespack – Photo by Cheryl Pursell

Damek Tomscha – Photo by Cheryl Pursell

Franklyn Kilome – Photo by Cheryl Pursell

Jeff Singer – Photo by Cheryl Pursell

Ranger Suarez – Photo from phillies.com

Corneluis Randolph – Photo by Gail Dull/Baseball Betsy

Luke Leftwich – Photo by Gail Dull/Baseball Betsy

Cole Irvin – photo from phillies.com

Seranthony Dominguez – photo from Phillies.com

Harold Arauz – Photo from Clearwater Threshers

Chapter Five: Season Recap – Lakewood BlueClaws

Jay Floyd wrote the following recap of the BlueClaws season. Jay manages and writes the website phoulbalz.com and is affiliated with the Shore Sports Network which covers the BlueClaws club.

Despite a roster loaded with considerable prospect names, the 2017 Lakewood BlueClaws saw a player that hadn't yet garnered hefty amounts of attention, first baseman Darick Hall, emerge as the team's premiere slugger and the story of the season for the Class-A Phillies affiliate.

Hall was such an offensive standout that not only was he valuable to the BlueClaws' lineup, he was also named the South Atlantic League's Most Valuable Player. The lefty batter turned 22 years old midway through the season and sported bust-out numbers with a .272 batting average, 28 doubles, a triple, 27 home runs (a team record) and 96 RBIs (another team record) in 114 games for Lakewood.

Hall, who was the Phils' 14th round draft choice in 2016, would close out his 2017 campaign with a week in the Advanced Class-A Florida State League playing for Clearwater.

Aside from his missile-like long balls, Hall's daily work and preparation are what impressed his BlueClaws coaches most. His presence in the lineup for a club that had several teenagers learning what minor league life was like proved crucial. Hall, who played three seasons of college ball, including his junior season with Dallas Baptist University, helped his teammates learn what the professional athlete life is all about. The six-foot-four, 234-pounder is a guy that can lead by example and he did just that all year long.

With many of the players on the BlueClaws roster in 2017 playing their first full season of professional ball, it was certainly a huge year, even for those that didn't post eye opening statistics. With the grind that is a 139-game schedule, the youngsters learned a lot about who they are and what it will take to improve and climb the developmental ladder in the minors.

Among the core group of talent that stood out on this BlueClaws team were 2016 top overall draft selection Mickey Moniak, Daniel Brito and Arquimedes Gamboa, who were all in their teens. Moniak, an outfielder, entered the season as an 18-year-old and had some struggles. With a few ups and downs, the lefty-hitting California native tallied a .236 average with five homers, 44 RBIs and 11 steals in 123 games.

Brito, a left-handed batting second baseman, sported similar numbers to Moniak with a .239 average, six home runs, 32 RBIs and 12 stolen bases as a 19-year-old in 112 contests.

Gamboa, a switch-hitting shortstop, missed time with an injury, but would notch a .261 batting average with six round trippers, 29 RBIs and eight steals through 79 games.

Adam Haseley, the Phillies' first round draft pick taken with the eighth overall selection in June, spent some time with Lakewood as well. The promising lefty batting outfielder would bat .258 with a homer and six RBIs in 18 games there.

On the mound the team's standout star was another name that doesn't get the kind of recognition normally tied to a top prospect. It was left-hander Nick Fanti and his pair of no hitters (he threw 8.2 hitless frames, getting help for the last out, on May 6 from Trevor Bettencourt and a full nine innings without allowing a safety on July 17) that made a huge splash and garnered plenty of buzz for the 'Claws throughout the year.

Fanti, a 31st round pick in 2015, stood out as a hurler beyond his years at age 20. He's got a mature approach, pitches fearlessly and has the ability to consistently throw strikes. In 21 starts, the Long Island, NY native tallied a 9-2 record with a 2.54 ERA and a 9.1 K/9 mark.

A collection of more highly ranked prospects were also part of the BlueClaws rotation in 2017. At the top of nearly everyone's list of Phillies minor leaguers to be excited about was righty pitcher Sixto Sanchez. The triple-digit-dealing Dominican opened the season as an 18-year-old and was sensational in his first turn in a full season league. He's an intelligent guy out there on the mound, knowing when to crank up the heat or when to lay off a bit to vary his velocity, which helps him stand out.

In eight starts following a stint on the disabled list with a neck strain, Sanchez posted a 1.67 ERA for Lakewood before being promoted to Clearwater to wrap up the final month of the season. In 18 total games he put together a 5-7 record with a 3.03 ERA and a .210 batting average against. Sanchez struck out 84 batters while walking just 18 in 95 innings.

JoJo Romero and Ranger Suarez were other pitchers that took the step up to Clearwater during the season and were each part of Lakewood's playoff chase in the first half, in which they fell just a half-game out of a playoff spot.

Romero recorded a 5-1 record with a 2.11 ERA and a 9.3 K/9 mark in 13 starts with Lakewood before he enjoyed similar success (5-2 record, 2.24 ERA, 8.4 K/9 in 10 games) with the Threshers. The left-hander was a fourth round draft selection by the Phillies in 2016.

Suarez, another lefty, would put together strong numbers as well with a 6-2 record, a 1.59 ERA, striking out an average of 9.5 per nine innings with a .177 batting average against. Following his promotion to Clearwater, Suarez, who turned 22 years old in August, went 3-4 with a 3.82 ERA in eight outings.

Adonis Medina was also a solid performer on the mound for Lakewood in 2017. The right-handed native of the Dominican Republic tosses a mid-to-high-90s fastball and posted a 4-9 record with a 3.01 ERA and a 10.0 K/9 mark through 22 starts. He may have as much of an upside as just about all the other pitching prospects in the Phils' system.

Reliever Will Hibbs led the South Atlantic League with 20 saves and posted a 0.75 WHIP and 1.77 ERA in 40 games (61 IP) with 73 K's as a dominant closer.

While the team didn't add to their collection of three South Atlantic League titles in 2017, the 'Claws continued to bring joy and excitement to the locals of the Jersey shore and surrounding areas.

Fresh off their first season failing to lead the Sally League in attendance after locking down that honor in each of their first 16 seasons, they'll be looking to get back on top in that category for the foreseeable future.

A newly formed group known as Shore Town Baseball acquired the operating interest of the BlueClaws in the summer of 2017. A Phillies affiliate since their inception in 2001, the BlueClaws have a player development deal in place that will leave them connected with Philadelphia through the 2020 season.

Here's a look at the "numbers" for 2017.

Win - Loss Record 73-66 overall (40-30 1st Half, 33-36 2nd Half) (38-30 Home, 35-36 Away)

3rd Place Overall - South Atlantic League Northern Division (7 team Division)

2nd Place - First Half and 5th Place - Second Half

Team Statistics: 14 team League

Hitting:

Runs - 12th - 543
Hits - 10th - 1,114
Doubles - 8th - 222
Triples - Tied for 4th - 32
Home Runs - 7th - 84
RBIs - 12th - 484
Total Bases - 8th - 1,652
Walks - 14th - 324

Least Strikeouts - 5th - 1,078
Stolen Bases - 10th - 92
OBP - 14th - .301
Slugging Pct. -9th - .360
Batting Average - Tied for 12th - .243
OPS - 12th - .661

Pitching:

ERA - 3rd - 3.26
Complete Games - Tied for 4th - 4
Shutouts - 1st - 22
Saves - 3rd - 36
IP - 5th - 1,208
Least Hits Allowed - 1st - 1,030
Least Runs Allowed - 2nd - 505
Least Earned Runs Allowed - 2nd - 438
Least Home Runs Allowed - 6th - 65
Least Hit Batters - Tied for 1st - 65
Least Walks - 5th - 363
Most Strikeouts - 4th - 1,231
WHIP - 1st - 1.15
Holds - 12th - 18

Individual League Leaders (Top 10 in League):

Hitting:
Games - Mickey Moniak - 8th - 123
Doubles - Darick Hall - 7th - 28
Triples - Mickey Moniak - Tied for 4th - 6
Home Runs - Darick Hall - 1st - 27
RBIs - Darick Hall - 1st - 96
Total Bases - Darick Hall - 1st - 227

Stolen Bases - Lucas Williams - 7th - 29
Slugging Percentage - Darick Hall - 1st - .533
OPS - Darick Hall - 1st - .87
Pitching:

Wins - McKenzie Mills - 1st - 12 (with Hagerstown), Nick Fanti - Tied for 4th - 9 and Alejandro Requena - 9 (with Asheville)
ERA (minimum 0.8 IP/league game) - Nick Fanti - 3rd - 2.54, Alejandro Requena - 5th - 2.74 (with Asheville), Bailey Falter - 7th - 2.99, Adonis Medina - 9th - 3.01
Games - Will Hibbs - Tied for 7th - 40
Starts - Adonis Medina - Tied for 6th - 22
Saves - Will Hibbs - 1st - 20, Trevor Bettencourt - Tied for 8th - 8
Strikeouts - Adonis Medina - 4th - 133, Nick Fanti - 5th - 121, McKenzie Mills - 6th - 118 (with Hagerstown)
WHIP (minimum 0.8 IP/league game) - Nick Fanti - 2nd - 0.91, Alejandro Requena - 4th - 1.05 (with Asheville)
Games Finished - Will Hibbs - 2nd - 36

Darick Hall – Photo taken by Jay Floyd

Sixto Sanchez – photo taken by Jay Floyd

Nick Fanti – photo taken by Jay Floyd

Mickey Moniak and Daniel Brito – photo by Jay Floyd

Will Hibbs – Photo by Gail Dull/Baseball Betsy

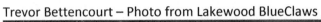
Trevor Bettencourt – Photo from Lakewood BlueClaws

Jonathan Hennigan

Jonathan's season was cut short by injury but he was having a promising year till then, he's got an outstanding curve ball and perhaps the best "spin rate" in the entire system.

Nick Fanti & Trevor Bettencourt combined on a no hitter on May 6th – Photo from Lakewood BlueClaws

Chapter Six – "It's All Part of It"

The Phillies minor league players adopted the slogan "It's All Part of it" to describe the grind of minor league baseball life. Jay Floyd wrote an article on April 25 that he published on his website Phoulbalz.com which further describes the slogan. Here's the article.

It's all part of it!

Are you wondering what that means? That's okay. You'll be in the know soon enough.

It's a simple saying that has become a slogan for baseball players for life inside and outside of the game. In a sport where its competitors are faced with an immense amount of failure while life presents similar outcomes at times, "It's All Part of It" has become an important adage for scores of players to lean on for reassurance and motivation.

"Whatever happens, the bus breaks down (or) you break a bat - hey, that's all part of it," Phillies outfield prospect Cord Sandberg excitedly shared in the home dugout of Lakewood's FirstEnergy Park recently.

Seems like an insightful thought process.

The motto has really caught on quite a bit and seems to be making an impression at multiple levels, in various organizations and even across continents.

The phrase "It's all part of it" or sometimes referred to as just "part" or "part-part" for short, was brought to the Phillies organization after outfield prospect Cord Sandberg and organization-mate third baseman Mitch Walding played alongside catcher Jack Murphy down under, in an off-season league.

"It spread down to Australia because I played down there in Canberra and we used to talk about it all the time," Murphy said. "Since there are a lot of guys from different organizations down there, the Phillies picked it up."

Murphy is a long-time Blue Jays minor leaguer and a Princeton University product that currently plays with Triple-A Oklahoma City in the Dodgers organization. When he was in the Toronto system, Murphy picked up the phrase from his manager Mike Redmond with Dunedin in the Florida State League in 2012. Redmond had adopted the mindset when he played for veteran skipper Jim Leyland during his time with the Marlins.

Redmond has since gone on to manage at the big-league level for Miami and coach in the majors for the Rockies.

A World Series and World Baseball Classic-winning manager's lessons getting passed down via a man that was virtually groomed to take on that skipper's duties, and then on to players that both men may never encounter sounds precisely how good coaching should work. Teach what matters and let those lessons thrive.

Murphy feels the sentiment has become a critical way of thinking for many players he has encountered.

"I mean, it's mostly a life motto for most of the guys," Murphy asserted. "The livelihood of playing can be a real grind. But when you say, 'Hey, it's all part of it!', you realize that's just how things are and keep going."

In addition to leaning on his faith, the 22-year-old Sandberg found peace of mind in the expression when he learned that he was going back a level to open the 2017 season after spending last year with Advanced Class-A Clearwater and playing with Lakewood two years back.

"We have a lot of talented guys that deserve to be where they're at. So, obviously, I was hoping to be in High A to start the year, but when Joe (Jordan) let me know that I was coming here and my at bats would be in Low A, I was like, 'Hey, that's all part of it.' I'm just going to come down here and do what I can to produce and show what I can do at this level and then let the rest just take care of itself," Sandberg said.

Phils corner infielder prospect Zach Green, currently sidelined with hip and elbow issues with Clearwater, has found solace in the phrase while dealing with repeated stints on the disabled list during his career.

"Injuries will happen. 0-for-4's. But, it's all part of it and that's why it shouldn't affect your character or confidence," said the 23-year-old Green.

It's all part of it may be bordering on sensational.

A great catchphrase these days is nothing without some manner to display your statement, so Sandberg and company have created t-shirts and are using the hashtag #PartPart on social networking sites.

The phrase has drawn the attention of Phillies developmental coaches, as Sandberg's manager with the BlueClaws and former big league infielder Marty Malloy has requested of Sandberg, "Where's my shirt? I want to be part of it!"

Malloy has grown fond of the outlook simply because of the way it can turn a negative into a positive for his players.

Also embracing the movement: Complete strangers.

"One night we went out in Tampa and we were all wearing our shirts and just random people would ask, 'What's all part of it?' And we would be like, 'Yeah, that's correct. You're right!' And they'd say, 'What do you mean, 'I'm right'?' 'It's whatever you want it to be. It's all part of it. Oh, you spilled your drink? It's all part of it.' And they were loving it, so I was able to get some more people on board," Sandberg explained, assuring me that part-part is for everyone, not just ball players.

So, how can you get down with the concept and be part of it?

"If anybody wants (a t-shirt), find me through social media, Twitter, Instagram or whatever and give me an address, a size and a color," Sandberg stated.

According to Murphy, though, a more ideal shopping option, a complete and proper website, should be coming soon.

But, don't worry about any delay on that front, everyone, because...well, you know why.

Phillies Minor Leaguers at a Tampa event during Spring
Training

Even old writers like myself are "part of it", here I'm with
Phillies President Andy MacPhail

Cord Sandberg – Photo by Cheryl Pursell

Chapter Seven - The Draft, International Signings and Trade Acquisitions

The annual Major League Baseball amateur draft began on June 12 this season, and the Phillies selected 40 players. Listed below are their 2017 draft selections.

1. Adam Haseley - OF - University of Virginia - from Windermere, Florida (Pick #8)

2. Spencer Howard - RHP - Cal Poly - from Templeton, California (Pick #45)

3. Conor Seabold - RHP -Cal State Fullerton - from Laguna Hills, California (Pick #83)

4. Jake Scheiner - 3B - University of Houston - from San Mateo, California (Pick #113)

5. Ethan Lindow - LHP - Locust Grove High School - from Locust Grove, Georgia - (Pick #143)

6. Dalton Guthrie - SS - University of Florida - from Sarasota, Florida (Pick #173)

7. Nick Maton - SS - Lincoln Land Community College - from Chatham, Illinois (Pick #203)

8. Jhordany Mezquita - LHP - No School - from Hazleton, Pennsylvania (Pick#233)

9. Jack Zoellner - 1B/3B - University of New Mexico - from Mesa, Arizona (Pick #263)

10. Connor Brogdon - RHP - Lewis Clark State - from Clovis, California (Pick #293)

11. Jake Holmes - SS - Pinnacle High School – from Pinnacle, Arizona (Pick #323)

12. David Parkinson - LHP - Ole Miss - JR- from Enrico, Virginia (Pick #353)

13. Colby Fitch - C - Louisville - from Rocheport, Missouri (Pick #383)

14. Zach Warren - LHP - Tennessee - from Vineland, New Jersey (Pick #413)

15. Alex Garcia - RHP - UC Santa Barbara - from Whittier, California (Pick #443)

16. Kyle Dohy - LHP - Cal Poly Pomona - from Covina, California (Pick #473)

17. Austin Listi - OF - Dallas Baptist University - from Huffman, Texas (Pick #503)

18. Damon Jones - LHP - Washington State University - from Twin Falls, Idaho (Pick #533)

19. Addison Russ - RHP - Houston Baptist University - from Amarillo, Texas (Pick #563)

20. Brady Schanuel - RHP- Parkland College - from Belleville, Illinois (Pick #593 - did not sign)

21. Jakob Hernandez - LHP - University of Texas-Arlington - from Georgetown, Texas (Pick #623)

22. Brian Mims - 2B - UNC Wilmington - from Montclair, Virginia (Pick #653)

23. Shane Drohan - LHP - Cardinal Newman HS - from West Palm Beach, Florida (Pick #683 - did not sign)

24. Kevin Markham - OF - University of Texas-San Antonio - from Willis, Texas (Pick #713)

25. Jesus Azuaje - SS - Glendale CC - from Buckeye, Arizona (Pick #743)

26. Quincy Nieporte - 1B - Florida State University - from Atlanta, Georgia (Pick #773)

27. Yahir Gurrola - OF - University of North Florida – from El Paso, Texas (Pick #803)

28. Bill Sullivan - RHP - St Marks High School – from Wilmington, Delaware (Pick #833 - did not sign)

29. Bailey Cummings - RHP - San Jacinto College North – from Pearland, Texas (Pick #863)

30. Matt Kroon - 3B - Central Arizona College - from Phoenix, Arizona (Pick #893 - did not sign)

31. Danny Mayer - OF - University of Pacific - from Downers Grove, Illinois (Pick #923)

32. Sati Santa Cruz - RHP - Central Arizona - from Tucson, Arizona (Pick #953)

33. Benjamin Brown - RHP - Ward Melville High School - from East Setauket, New York (Pick #983)

34. Kyle Hurt - RHP - Torrey Pines High School – from San Diego, California (Pick #1,013 - did not sign)

35. Brian Morrell - RHP - Shoreham Wading River High School - from Wading River, New York (Pick #1,043 - did not sign)

36. Joe Breaux - OF - McLennan Community College – from Waco, Texas (Pick #1,073 - did not sign

37. Edouard Julien - 2B - Cardinal Roy Secondary School - from Quebec, Canada (Pick #1,103 - did not sign)

38. Landon Gray - C - Weatherford College - from Cresson, Texas (Pick #1,133 - did not sign)

39. D.J. Stewart - 3B - Westminster Christian Academy High School – from Chesterfield, Missouri (Pick #1,163)

40. Paul Coumoulos - OF - Bishop McLaughlin Catholic High School – from Springfield, FL (Pick #1,193 - did not sign)

The club was able to sign 30 of the 40 selected and the young men began their pro careers with a mini camp in Clearwater followed by assignments to various affiliated teams to compete. Most were assigned to short season squads where they spent their entire first season.

Adam Haseley in his 1st pro game – Photo by Mark Wylie

Austin Listi – Photo by Mark Wylie

Jake Holmes – Photo by Mark Wylie

Ben Brown – Photo by Mark Wylie

Yahir Gurrola – Photo by Mark Wylie

The International signing period for 2017 began in July and the Phillies were very active during the month. Their international signings included the following players as reported by Baseball America:

- Luis Garcia, SS, Dominican Republic (#12 prospect)

- Victor Vargas, RHP, Colombia (# 25 prospect)

- Carlos Betancourt, RHP, Venezuela (#41 prospect)

- Cesar Rodriguez, C, Venezuela (#42 prospect)

- Alfonso Puello, RHP, Dominican Republic

- Oscar Gonzalez, C, Venezuela

- Cristian Hernandez, RHP, Venezuela

- Alejandro Made, RHP, Dominican Republic

- Alberto Torres, LHP, Colombia

- Diego Tamariz, RHP, Venezuela

Victor Vargas – Photo by Mark Wylie

Alfonso Puello – Photo by Mark Wylie

At the July trade deadline and again during the month of August the Phillies acquired even more young Minor League talent as they traded big league veterans Howie Kendrick, Pat Neshek, Jeremy Hellickson, Joaquin Benoit and Juan Nicasio. Here's a listing of the young players they acquired in return.

Garrett Cleavinger - LHP - 23 years old – acquired from Orioles in exchange for Hellickson

McKenzie Mills - LHP - 21 years old – acquired from Nationals in exchange for Howie Kendrick

Jose Gomez – SS – 20 years old – acquired from Rockies in exchange for Pat Neshek

Alejandro Requena RHP – 21 years old – acquired from Rockies in exchange for Pat Neshek

JD Hammer – RHP – 23 years old – acquired from Rockies in exchange for Pat Neshek

Eliezar Alvarez – 2B – 22 years old – acquired from Cardinals in exchange for Juan Nicasio

Seth McGarry – RHP – 23 years old – acquired from Pirates in exchange for Joaquin Benoit

Chapter Eight - Season Recap – Williamsport Cross Cutters

Pat Borders managed the club for the third time this season and was assisted by Pitching Coach Hector Berrios along with first year Hitting Coach Tyler Henson.

It was a relatively young team this year with the average age of 20.18 years old for the 33 players listed on the roster at year end, including 19 Pitchers with an average age of 20.42 years old and 14 Position Players with an average age of 19.86 years old. This year's team also had some standout talent, as Mitch Rupert of the Williamsport Sun Gazette stated it was in his opinion the most talented Williamsport team he has covered. The team employed 23 different position players this summer and 22 Pitchers.

Here's a look at the "numbers" for 2017.

Win - Loss Record 37-37 (22-16 at home and 15-21 away)

Fourth Place in Pinckney Division of New York Penn League

Team Statistics: 14 team League

Hitting:

10th in Runs Scored - 283
8th in Hits - 587
Tied for 1st in Doubles - 133
8th in Triples - 17
2nd in Home Runs - 45
9th in RBIs - 250
5th in Total Bases - 889
14th in Walks - 199
Tied for 3rd in Least Strikeouts - 600

Tied for 8th in Stolen Bases - 51
10th in OBP - .312
1st in Slugging Pct. - .367
Tied for 5th in Batting Average - .242
3rd in OPS - .678

Pitching:

8th in ERA - 3.43
2nd in Saves - 24
8th in IP - 642.1
7th in Least Hits Allowed - 554
Tied for 6th in Least Runs Allowed - 290
Tied for 7th in Least Earned Runs Allowed - 251
Tied for 3rd in Least HR Allowed - 22
13th in Least Walks Allowed - 281
4th in Most Strikeouts - 688
Tied for 6th in WHIP - 1.30
Tied for 3rd in Holds - 22

Individual League Leaders (Top 10 in League):

Hitting:

Games Played - Josh Stephen - 64 (3rd), Greg Pickett - 62
(tied for 5th), Jake Scheiner - 61 (tied for 6th)
At Bats - Josh Stephen - 239 (5th, Jake Scheiner - 236 (8th)
Runs - Nick Maton -34 (Tied for 6th), Jake Scheiner - 32 (Tied
for 7th)
Hits - Greg Pickett - 60 (Tied for 9th), Josh Stephen & Jake
Scheiner - 59 (Tied for 8th)

Doubles - Malvin Matos & Jhailyn Ortiz - 15 (Tied for 4th), Jake Scheiner - 14 (Tied for 5th), Josh Stephen - 12 (Tied for 7th), Greg Pickett - 11 (Tied for 8th)

Triples - Josh Stephen - 5 (3rd), Rodolfo Duran - 3 (Tied for 5th)

Home Runs - Jhailyn Ortiz & Cole Stobbe - 8 (Tied for 3rd), Greg Pickett - 6 (Tied for 4th), Jake Scheiner - 4 (Tied for 6th)

RBIs - Jhailyn Ortiz - 30 (Tied for 9th)

Total Bases - Jhailyn Ortiz, Greg Pickett, Jake Scheiner - 89 (Tied for 10th)

Walks - Nick Maton - 30 (Tied for 7th)

Strikeouts - Greg Pickett - 70 (Tied for 6th), Cole Stobbe - 67 (Tied for 8th)

Slugging Percentage - Jhailyn Ortiz - .560 (1st)

Pitching:

Wins - Kyle Young - 7 (Tied for 3rd), Will Stewart, Julian Garcia, Andrew Brown - 4 (Tied for 6th), Connor Brogdon - 3 (Tied for 7th)

ERA (min .8 IP per League Game) - Kyle Young - 2.77 (10th)

Games - Luis Ramirez - 23 (Tied for 1st), Randy Alcantara - 19 (Tied for 5th), Connor Brogdon, Jhon Nunez, Zach Warren - 16 (Tied for 8th)

Starts - Julian Garcia, Kyle Young, Will Stewart - 13 (Tied for 3rd), Andrew Brown - 10 (Tied for 6th), Spencer Howard - 9 (Tied for 7th)

Saves - Luis Ramirez - 11 (1st), Randy Alcantara - 5 (Tied for 6th), Connor Brogdon & Damon Jones - 3 (Tied for 8th)

Strikeouts - Julian Garcia - 82 (2nd), Kyle Young - 72 (8th)

WHIP (min .8 IP per League Game) - Kyle Young - 1.12 (9th)

Holds - Randy Alcantara - 4 (Tied for 3rd), Connor Brogdon & David Parkinson - 3 (Tied for 4th), Kyle Dohy, Orestes Melendez, Jake Kelzer & Zach Warren - 2 (Tied for 6th)
Games Finished - Luis Ramirez - 18 (1st), Randy Alcantara - 10 (Tied for 8th)

Beyond the Numbers:

Jhailyn Ortiz had a standout year before succumbing to injury at the end of the season. The 18-year-old put up very impressive numbers hitting .302 in 159 at bats which would have been among the league leaders if he had attained the minimum qualifying number of at bats. He showed impressive speed for a big guy (6'3" 215), fielding skills as a Right-fielder (excellent arm) and tremendous power. This young man has a real chance at becoming a special player as he advances.

Greg Pickett showed good offensive skills and power but the 20-year-old has a ways to go as a fielder. He was moved to first base last fall and works hard to improve but will have to get better to hold down a full time defensive position there.

Jake Scheiner (22-year-old fourth round pick in this year's draft) showed all around skills as a potential super utility player aka Ben Zobrist. That's the projection for him, he's got very good offensive skills and is a gamer as he played a good deal of the season with a nagging hamstring issue. He's an Utley type mentality it would seem, good guy to have, a smart player.

Josh Stephen (19-year-old 2016 11th round pick) turned his early season struggles around and was 7-for-17 in his last three games. He's a "Pro Hitter" type, reminiscent of Andrew Pullin, that I feel has a very bright future. Look for him to breakout in 2018.

Adam Haseley (21-year-old 2017 first round pick) was solid in his 37 games at Williamsport hitting .270/.350/.380 before moving up to Lakewood. He wore down as the season progressed as he also had played a full college schedule. With a restful offseason he likely starts next summer at Clearwater, very good all-around skills.

Cole Stobbe (20-year-old 2016 third round pick) and Luis Encarnacion (20-year-old international signee from 2013) both had their struggles this season but there's a heavy financial investment in them and both are still very young players. They will likely continue in the offseason training and conditioning program and hopefully use this summer as a learning experience.

Kyle Young (19-year-old 22nd round draft pick from 2016) had a breakout season and has a very bright future. The seven-foot lefty should see his velocity increase as he progresses and gets stronger. He too could become a very special player. One to watch.

Connor Seabold (21-year-old third round 2017 pick) and Spencer Howard (21-year-old 2017 second round pick) both showed in limited appearances (due to extended college seasons) flashes of real upside. Both are big arms and likely anchor the Lakewood rotation to start next season.

Randy Alcantara (20 years old), Luis Ramirez (19 years old), Connor Brogdon (22 years old), Damon Jones (22 years old),

Zach Warren (21 years old) and David Parkinson (21 years old) all had solid seasons as relievers. Ramirez seems akin to Pedro Beato in how he pitches, and the others show power stuff with big strikeout ratios. Jones, Parkinson and Brogdon project as mid 90's FB range and Alcantara has a mix of pitches that make him akin to Mark Leiter Jr. They should at the least start the year in Lakewood next summer.

Julian Garcia (22 years old), Will Stewart (20 years old) and Andrew Brown (19 years old) had solid seasons as starters. Spring training should determine their 2018 placement with bullpen roles also a possibility.

The sleeper of the staff is Ramon Rosso, he's 21 and worked his way up three levels this summer. He has a plus FB I'm told as he tallied 105 K's this summer in 75 2/3 IP. He's also got good size at 6'4" 215 and could be a young man who moves up multi levels again next summer.

Good season for our short schedule boys at Williamsport, good things ahead for them.

Me with Randy Alcantara in Spring Training – Photo by Stu Blanton

Jhailyn Ortiz – Photo by Mark Wylie during Fall Instructs

Kyle Young – photo taken by Mark Wylie during Fall Instructs

Greg Pickett – photo taken by Mark Wylie during Fall
Instructs

Josh Stephen – photo taken by Mark Wylie during Fall
Instructs

Adam Haseley – Photo taken by Mark Wylie – Fall Instructs

Raymond Rosso – Photo taken by Mark Wylie – Fall Instructs

Connor Brogdon – Photo from Williamsport CrossCutters

Chapter Nine – Gulf Coast League Phillies

Jim Peyton wrote the recap for the Gulf Coast League Phillies. Jim is the primary writer for PhuturePhilies.com and is a daily observer at the Carpenter Complex for the Gulf Coast Phillies. He's also the beat writer for the Clearwater Threshers. Here's Jim's recap for the 2017 GCL Phillies.

I spend a lot of time watching Phillies' prospects as they pass through Clearwater. One of the things I have learned, and it is something that I hope others will consider, is that the Gulf Coast League is a rookie league where the indoctrination of young men into their chosen profession of baseball and the development of their talents are more important that the results on a score board or in a box score.

Each June, high school and college players the Phillies signed after their selection during the annual amateur draft, report to the Phillies' Paul Owens Training Facility at the Carpenter Complex in Clearwater. They begin their careers physically more advanced than their Latin American counterparts, but slightly behind developmentally. Most of the Latin players have spent a season on the roster of one of the Phillies' summer teams in the Dominican Summer League. The few who weren't on one of the Dominican teams would have spent months at the Phillies' Dominican Academy that shares facilities with the DSL teams.

When the Phillies' Gulf Coast League team gathers at the Complex, it brings together this diverse group of individuals. The Phillies as an organization resist the urge to make major changes in a new player's approach. Their philosophy is to allow the newest players, the drafted players, to continue doing the things in the ways they have grown comfortable.

The Phillies wait until the fall instructional league to break down and rebuild their baseball mechanics.

In addition to these hurdles, the 2017 Gulf Coast League Phillies had a tough act to follow. The 2016 team, posted the best regular season record (43-15, .741) with the league's youngest team, won a first-round playoff series against the Braves, and extended the Cardinals to the penultimate game in the three-game championship series.

The 2016 team's hitters posted a league best .342 OBP, .390 SLG, .732 OPS, 294 runs, 514 hits, and 109 doubles. They were led by Lenin Rodriguez (.340), Mickey Moniak (.284, 28 RBI), Daniel Brito (.284, 25 RBI), Jhailyn Ortiz (.231, 8 HR, 27 RBI), Cole Stobbe (.270, 4 HR, 13 RBI), and Josh Stephen (.253, 26 RBI).

The 2016 team's pitching staff posted the league's best team ERA (2.51), allowed the fewest runs/earned runs (178/142), the lowest WHIP (1.117), and issued the second fewest walks (146). They chalked up some impressive individual numbers: starters - Sixto Sanchez (5-0, 0.50, 54.0 IP, 8 BB, 44 K, 0.76 WHIP), Nick Fanti (7-0, 1.57, 51.2 IP, 65 K, 9 BB, 0.87 WHIP), and Mauricio Llovera (7-1, 1.87, 53.0 IP, 12 BB, 56 K, 0.96 WHIP); swing man - Luis Carrasco (7-2, 2.18, 41.1 IP, 14 BB, 50 K, 1.19 WHIP); Kyle Young (3-0, 2.67, 9 G, 27.0 IP, 2 BB, 19 K, 0.93 WHIP); closers - Tyler Frohwirth (1-1, 2.08, 10 saves) and Jose Nin (1-1, 1.02, 7 saves); and Andrew Brown (0-0, 2.75, 11 G, 19.2 IP, 5 BB, 20 K, 1.17 WHIP).

Clearly, the bar was set high for 2017 team. All they did was meet expectations with a league-best regular season record

(36-22, .621) and another trip to the post season where they lost to the eventual champion, Yankees East. The hitters posted a league best .267 AVG, .378 SLG, .718 OPS, 310 runs, 517 hits, and struck out a league low 313 times. The pitching staff posted the league's second-best team ERA (3.05), and allowed the fewest runs/earned runs (205/166). Manuel Silva tied for the league lead in wins with 6 and Ben Pelletier was third in the league with a .333 batting average.

The 2017 GCL Phillies played well to start the season, but had an 11-10 record after extending to a four-game losing streak after losing the first game of a double header on July 22nd. They bounced back in the second game and went on a seven-game winning streak, outscoring their opponents 45-12. They had made up half of the four games they had trailed the first-place Blue Jays.

The Phillies continued to win games and stalk the Blue Jays until a win on August 15 forged a tie for first place. They took over sole possession of first place the next day and remained there for the remainder of the season. They did drop into a one-day tie on the 19th, but opened up their largest lead of 3.5 games on the 28th, and clinched the division title on the following day with three games remaining on the schedule.

These Phillies were clutch down the stretch. They went 6-1 in head-to-head match ups with the Blue Jays in August/September, and were 8-2 against them for the season, outscoring them 57-23 and shutting them out twice (they had 8 shut outs during the season). They were only shut out once themselves, albeit in their playoff game.

That's all well and good, but as I stated above, the Gulf Coast League is a rookie league where development is more important than winning. When you can do both, great! The 2017 Phillies did not have big name prospects like the 2016 group that included Mickey Moniak, Kevin Gowdy, Cole Stobbe, Daniel Brito, Jhailyn Ortiz, and Sixto Sanchez. What the 2017 group did have was a group of talented kids who played well together. Among them, some stood out.

Starting Pitchers

Jhordany Mezquita, the Phillies eighth round pick in the 2017 draft, is a pitcher to keep an eye on. He signed an international free agent contract in March that the major league office voided due to his residency in Hazelton, Pennsylvania. He signed for the same amount in June, saving the Phillies a little slot money as an added bonus. The 19-year old LHP has a high 80s-mid 90s fastball and a couple of nice secondary pitches that could accelerate his trajectory through the lower levels of the organization. But, since 2017 was his first season of professional ball, and since he only pitched 37.2 innings, he'll likely be in short season again.

Francisco Morales has a great baseball body. At 6'4, 185 lbs., he's got the size and the frame to handle more weight/muscle. The 18-year old RHP signed as an international free agent in 2016 and spent the summer at the Dominican Academy before coming stateside for Instructs that fall. This season was his first professional season. He already has a mid-90s fastball. Though the youngster displays occasional control issues with a 4.4 BB/9, he tantalizes with a 9.6 K/9. After just 41.1 GCL innings, he'll likely be in short-season again next year.

Manuel Silva quietly put together a nice season. The slightly built LHP throws in the low 90s. He's a skinny 18-year-old and will likely be part of the Phillies weight program this fall, although he doesn't look like he has the frame to hold the necessary weight/muscle. He put together a 6-0 record with a 2.60 ERA in 45.0 innings. However, I wouldn't be surprised if he repeats Rookie ball next season. He spent Instructs on crutches

Ethan Lindow is a promising LHP, drafted by the Phillies in the fifth round of the 2017 First Year draft. He had an upper 80s fastball as part of a three-pitch mix that includes a curve ball and changeup. He had an 11.1 K/9, highest among starters. He tossed 27.2 innings. I saw Lindow in an Instructs appearance where he struck out five in 2.0 innings.

Relief Pitchers

Jakob Hernandez was the Phillies 21st round selection in the 2017 Amateur Draft. He's a big kid, built like a football lineman. Several baseball sites agree that he is 6'4, but from there differ. The Phillies listed him as 275 lbs. on draft day. Baseball Reference and MiLB list him as 260, but the Phillies had him at 290 on their Instructional League roster. No matter, the kid can pitch. The LHP was a starter for UT-Arlington. He earned second-team All-Sun Belt Conference honors, went 6-1 with a 3.28 ERA in 13 starts, tossing one complete game, and hurled 79.2 innings, striking out a team-leading 89. He went 5-0 with a 1.53 ERA in his five road starts, and defeated #20 Louisiana. His only loss came against ranked Coastal Carolina (#29). The Phillies used him in a relief role and limited him to 11 innings, I believe due to his heavy pitch counts in college (he often surpassed 100 pitches in a game). Hernandez possesses a "killer", overhand curve. He struck out 8 of the first 9 batters he faced, and didn't allow a base runner until his fifth appearance. He finished with a win, a save, a 1.64 ERA, 0.818 WHIP, 0 BB and 15 K (12.3/9 IP). He was working on a change up in Instructs. I would not be surprised if the Phillies used him as a starter next season.

Anton Kuznetsov was signed as an international free agent on September 8, 2016. The LHP hails from Moscow, Russia. He was assigned to one of the DSL teams and invited stateside for minor league spring training. He impressed coaches so much that he was reassigned to the GCL Phillies prior to the Amateur Draft. He has a mid-80s to upper-80s fastball and a couple of raw off-speed pitches. But he keeps the ball down and throws strikes. He led the team with 5 saves, allowed just one earned run, posted a 0.36 ERA, walked 4 and struck out 24 in 25.1 innings. When I first saw Kuznetsov pitch, I thought he looked a little stiff, like he was following a series of steps on the mound, sort of like learning to pitch from a book titled "Pitching for Dummies". By August, he looked smooth on the mound, and I stopped being surprised at how well he pitched.

Middle Infielders

Brayan Gonzalez was signed as an international free agent on July 2, 2016. He was part of a middle infielder class that included Christian Valerio, Leandro Medina, Jose Tortolero, Edgar Made, Nicolas Torres, Luiggi Mujica, and Juan Herrera. Gonzalez stood out during Instructs, and while the rest started their careers in the Dominican Republic, he started his at second base for the GCL Phillies. Gonzalez handled himself well at the plate despite giving up 2.5 years to opposing pitchers. And he made the transition from shortstop to second, committing just 5 errors in 38 games.

Jonathan Guzman was signed as an international free agent on August 17, 2015. He debuted in the DSL in 2015 and hit .300 in 277 plate appearances. He teamed with Gonzalez during 2016 Instructs and they played well as a middle infield pairing. They continued to play together giving the Phillies a formidable middle infield. Guzman started the season in Williamsport but returned after the June Amateur Draft in time for the start of the GCL season. He also played a game for the Threshers in the Florida State League.

Dalton Guthrie was drafted by the Phillies in the sixth round of the 2017 First Year draft out of Florida. He was a key part of the Gators' run to their College World Series victory. The shortstop is the son of former major league pitcher Mark Guthrie. Guthrie was limited to a handful of GCL games due to injury, but looks sharp on the field. His bat will dictate how quick he moves through the organization. I had a brief talk with Phillies' scout Johnny Almarez who spoke effusively about his future.

Corner Infielders

Quincy Nieporte was drafted by the Phillies in the 26th round of the 2017 Amateur Draft out of Florida State. He led the country with 82 RBI his senior year. The first baseman represented the power in the GCL Phillies line up. He led the team with 5 HR and 35 RBI. He had a .299 batting average with a team-leading .494 SLG and .848 OPS. He walked 12 times and struck out 17 times in 180 plate appearances.

Jake Holmes was drafted by the Phillies in the 11th round of the 2017 Amateur Draft out of high school. He's 6'3, 195 lbs. and looked out of place at shortstop. But, he is a rangy fielder with a good arm. Offensively, he showed an ability to lay off the pitcher's pitch and flashed some power. He hit both of his home runs in the same game, and both cleared the scoreboard on Robin Roberts Field easily. I was not surprised when he was moved to third base at the beginning of Instructs.

Outfielders

Ben Pelletier was drafted by the Phillies in the 34th round of the 2015 Amateur Draft while he was still in the Canadian equivalent of high school. He signed on July 15, 2015 and spent the next 6 weeks at the Complex until he returned to school at the end of the summer. He was assigned to the GCL Phillies in June of 2016, and reported to the team after graduation. His somewhat late arrival and a platoon that saw him in just 27 games delayed his development. Pelletier came into his own this season, leading the team with his .333 batting average. He was second on the team with 3 HR and 26 RBI.

Simon Muzziotti was signed as a free agent by the Phillies on July 5, 2016 after Major League Baseball invalidated his contract with the Boston Red Sox, a penalty for their violating international signing rules. He switched DSL teams and saw his average drop about .080 points. However, he impressed enough in 2017 spring training to earn an assignment to the

GCL Phillies. He played almost exclusively in center field and committed just one error. Offensively, he led off and posted a .269 average. He puts the ball in play. in 141 plate appearances, he walked 7 times and struck out eight. He has better-than-average speed and isn't averse to dropping a bunt when the situation presents itself.

Catchers

Rafael Marchan is a promising young catcher who was signed as an international free agent on July 3, 2015. He spent that summer at the Phillies' Venezuelan Academy before being assigned to one of the Phillies' DSL teams in June of 2016. While at the academy, he was converted from shortstop to catcher. Despite his short time at the position, Marchan shows remarkable catching instincts. He threw out 43% of attempted base stealers. At the plate, he makes decent contact and puts the ball in play (only 4 BB and 8 K in 93 plate appearances), but his average plummeted from .333 to .238 with his move stateside this year. Marchan lost the first two weeks of the season when he was spiked in a play at the plate in the season opener.

Others who caught my eye include Phillies first round pick Adam Haseley who hit .583 in 14 plate appearances before reporting to Williamsport, Yahir Gurrola who hit .333 and stole 12 bases in 126 plate appearances before being promoted to Williamsport, Keudy Bocio who hit .278 with 22 runs and 18 RBI and seemed to be involved in every rally down the stretch, Jesus Henriquez who played flawless defense in his portion of the second base platoon, Kevin Markham who played three outfield positions and drew 22 walks against 9 strike outs, Phillies 39th round pick D.J.

Stewart who signed late out of high school and played sparingly, Ramon Rosso who struck out 13 in 9.0 innings on his way from the DSL to Williamsport, Ben Brown who is from the same portion of Long Island that produced Nick Fanti and Kyle Young, and fellow pitchers Denny Martinez, Victor Sobil, Oscar Marcelino.

Manuel Silva – Photo taken by Gail Dull/Baseball Betsy

Jakob Hernandez – photo taken by Jim Peyton

Francisco Morales – Photo taken by Gail Dull/Baseball Betsy

Quincy Nieporte – Photo taken by Gail Dull/Baseball Betsy

Ben Pelletier – Photo taken by Gail Dull/Baseball Betsy

Ethan Lindow – Photo taken by Mark Wylie

Simon Muzziotti – Photo by Mark Wylie

Chapter Ten – Dominican Summer League Phillies

The Phillies fielded two teams in the Dominican Summer League, named Team Red and Team White. It's hard to ascertain how the young players are developing in the Dominican as there's no video to watch, limiting our reviews to purely statistical aspects, in addition to what we can see when the young men come over to the U.S. if they are promoted. With that said, here's my review of the 2017 DSL Phillies.

Team Red finished the Dominican Summer League season 32-39 under Manager Waner Santana and his coaches Les Straker (Pitching) and Samuel Hiciano (Hitting). The average age of the team's 38-player final roster was 18.26 years old.

Hitting:

The club finished with a team average of .234 scoring 279 runs on 515 hits including 102 doubles, 22 triples and 9 home runs. They amassed 688 total bases with 226 walks and struck out 446 times. They stole quite a few bases (127) which was 5th best amongst the 39 clubs in the DSL. Their OBP/SLG/OPS line was .318/.312/.630. The average age of the position players on the team's final roster was 17.67 (15 players).

18-year-old Jose Rivera led the team in batting average (.284 - 29 for 102), OBP (.432) and OPS (.765) while 18-year-old catcher Carlos Oropeza leading in at bats (217), hits (57) and Total Bases (75). Young 17-year-old shortstops Edgar Made (.346 OBP) and Christian Valerio (.345 OBP) had solid initial seasons offensively however Valerio struggled defensively committing 24 errors.

Pitching:

The team ERA was 3.57 in 600 2/3 IP with a WHIP of 1.38. They struck out 483 batters while walking 261. The bullpen had 20 saves and 12 holds. The average age of the 23 pitchers listed on the roster was 18.65.

18-year-old right-hander Leonel Aponte went 7-1 in 14 games (12 starts) with an outstanding 0.84 ERA and 0.78 WHIP in 75 1/3 IP. He struck out 66 batters and walked just 9.

20-year-old righty Ludovico Coveri had a very good season posting a 1.54 ERA in 24 games (53 2/3 IP) with a 6-4 record, he had 5 saves and finished 16 games.

17-year-old Jose Conopoima posted a 2.04 ERA in 35 1/3 IP while 17-year-old Victor Santos went 4-2 with a 2.57 ERA in 49 IP. Both are right-handers.

Team White finished the Dominican Summer League season 45-26 under Manager Orlando Munoz and his coaches Alex Concepcion (Pitching) and Homy Ovalles (Hitting). Team White also has an Assistant Pitching Coach (Feliberto Sanchez) and an Infield Coach (Silverio Navas). The average age of the team's final roster was 18.62 (37 players)

Hitting:

The team's batting average of .261 (588 for 2,249) was 4th best in the league. They scored 299 runs and had 75 doubles, 36 triples and 11 home runs. They had 768 total bases, walked 183 times and struck out 414 times. They stole 109 bases, had a .327 OBP, .341 slugging percentage and a .669 OPS. The average age of the position players on the final roster was 18.07 (15 players)

18-year-old catcher Juan Mendez hit .379 in 140 at bats with an OBP of .411, slugging percentage of .571 and OPS of .982. Those all led the club.

The team had 6 players with more than 200 at bats led by Alexito Feliz with 247. 17-year-old Nicolas Torres had a great first year leading the club with 80 hits and hitting .333 with an OBP of .383 and an OPS of .804. He also led the team in doubles with 13

19-year-old center fielder Julio Francisco led the team in triples (10 - also led the league), stolen bases (22), total bases (107), walks (28) and runs (51). He hit .318/.399/.442 with an OPS of .841 in 242 at bats.

The 21-year-old Feliz led the team in Home Runs (4) and RBIs (35). He had a solid season hitting .296

Pitching:

The team posted a 3.21 ERA in 603 IP. They led the league in strikeouts with 592 and issued 256 walks. The club had a 1.29 WHIP. Their bullpen crew had 21 saves and 14 holds. The pitching staff's average age was 19 (22 players).

21-year-old righty Raymond Rosso went 6-1 with an 0.74 ERA in 48 2/3 IP and was promoted to the GCL Phillies and then subsequently to Williamsport. He struck out 69 batters while he was on Team White.

Carlos Salazar had 6 saves to lead the club and posted a 1.57 ERA in 46 IP.

20-year-old right-hander Bryan Alcala went 6-2 with an ERA of 2.15 in 67 IP with 53 k's

Juan Francisco – Photo by Mark Wylie

Chapter Eleven - Florida Instructional League

Each year the Phillies developmental season wraps up with what's known as the Florida Instructional League. Lower level players in the system are invited to a mini camp in Clearwater which simulates spring training and is used both as a teaching session and an acclimation of what's to come the following spring. Each of the Spring Grapefruit League teams hold camps and games are scheduled with other organizations just as they are in spring training. This year's camp was cut short due to impacts of the hurricane that hit Florida in September, but the club was still able to get a few weeks of work in. Here are some observations from the camp as my wife and I attended both games and workouts.

Pitchers:

There were 35 guys officially listed on the active FIL roster and a few more were there on rehab assignments. Some of the guys didn't pitch in games as they were invited to work on things individually with the coaches on the side, while also getting acclimated with the Phillies training regimen.

Sixto Sanchez - the just turned 19 years old has big time talent, that's very evident. Hopefully he stays humble and hungry as he continues to progress through the system. I only saw him pitch two innings during FIL, what was noticeable was he seemed to be focusing on command and delivery with a softer landing in mind. The baseball jumps out of his hand regardless.

Kyle Young - another 19-year-old who has a shot at being a very special pitcher. The seven-footer has a smooth and repeatable delivery and doesn't sling the ball due as one might expect due to his height but rather has a 3/4 motion with an out-front release that with his stride seems to come beyond the front part of the mound. He will be back in Clearwater during the offseason for continued strength training. As he adds velocity to the fastball this young man has top of the rotation skills from the left-hand side. He and Sanchez could be anchors to a very good pitching staff in the 2020s.

Ethan Lindow - 18-year-old lefty who I saw pitch for the first time in FIL against the Braves. He was smooth and compact and has good movement with his pitches. He also was very composed on the bump. In the game I saw he struck out 5 batters in 2 innings and did so mostly with a fastball that had both sink and tail to it. His FB sits low 90's right now but the 6'3" 180 pounder has room to grow with that as he adds strength and maturity. He too will be back in Clearwater during the offseason for strength training. Good looking young pitcher.

Both Spencer Howard and Jhordany Mezquita threw in games I watched. They each have easy deliveries and excellent ball movement. Both young men should be key rotation pieces next summer on full season squads I would think, both have big upside. I look forward to seeing them pitch again this spring.

Jakob Hernandez, Connor Brogdon, David Parkinson, Damon Jones, Zach Warren and Kyle Dohy are college draftees who showed various styles. Hernandez comes straight over the top as a lefty and has a 12 to 6 curve ball, he's not a hard thrower but ball movement is excellent.

Brogdon, Parkinson and Jones are all capable of mid 90's heaters from what I saw during FIL play. Dohy and Warren are low 90's FB lefties who pitch to contact more from what I saw, both use more secondary pitches as relievers.

Young studs: I saw three kids throw once each, they are all just 16 years old and were just signed this past summer. Their names are Carlos Bettencourt, Victor Vargas and Alfonso Puello. Each showed poise beyond their youthful age in the intra-squad scrimmage I saw them pitch in. I would think each of them plays in the GCL next summer, names to pay attention to for sure.

Don't forget about these guys: Ben Brown, Francisco Morales, Leonel Aponte and Jose Jimenez each have upside to expand upon. Brown is an 18-year-old who's 6'6" 210 and has a frame that with added muscle projects to a big-league build. His fastball is presently sitting mid to high 80s but that should increase with better mechanics and strength, he will also be back in Clearwater in the offseason for strength training. Morales has all the tools to be a special pitcher, the 17-year-old already has a mid-90s fast ball and throws three off speed pitches in addition. He's a big kid at 6'4" 185 and is probably not yet done growing. Was off on command the one time I saw him in Dunedin against the Blue Jays but battled through it, another good quality. Jimenez and Aponte are off the radar guys, but I like each young man's makeup and approach. I've only seen them each throw a couple times, but it certainly was enough to want to see more, I think they could develop into solid prospects.

Catchers:

Two guys stood out to me, Henri Lartigue and Rodolfo Duran. Duran made a spectacular play in a game against the Yankees with runners on first and third. He threw out the would be base stealer at second base and caught a short hop throw back to the plate from the second baseman to tag the runner out who had broken from third and complete a double play. The young man has a canon and can also run as I saw him leg out a triple in the same game. Lartigue was impressive during both weeks of FIL with his blocking, field command and receiving skills.

Infield:

Both Jake Holmes and DJ Stewart are works in progress as third baseman, but each teenager has potential. I'd expect them both to be on GCL rosters next summer, and rumblings are the Phillies will have two GCL teams, so it wouldn't be a surprise if each is the designated starter on the two separate teams. Raw talents.

Greg Pickett had an excellent FIL Camp, he looks ready to move ahead to full season play at Lakewood and it wouldn't be a surprise if Quincy Nieporte joins him there as a 1B/DH combo. Both hit the ball really well. Danny Mayer also could see some first base time.

Arquimedes Gamboa and Jonathan Guzman are smooth fielders at short stop. Both bigger kids as well, they need to prove they can hit but the gloves are there, as are the arms to be excellent defenders.

Luis Garcia looked a bit timid in his first U.S. pro camp experience. The 17-year-old should be back next spring in for XST and GCL as a shortstop.

Brayan Gonzalez plays with a lot of confidence at second base, good quick bat also it seems, nice looking player.

Outfield:

Jhailyn Ortiz is a special player, he's one of those guys who when he's at the plate everyone watches. The 18-year-old has tremendous bat speed and ball really takes off when he hits it. He also stands close to the plate and got hit a few times this week, he was also hit a lot at Williamsport. He's likely destined to play at Lakewood next summer, and it will be very interesting to see how he does in full season play.

Austin Listi and Danny Mayer both hit the ball well in FIL play and showed versatility also by logging some innings at first base. I could see both with chances to make the Clearwater roster next spring.

Josh Stephen hit the ball consistently well and was more focused on pulling the ball to right field it seemed. I like his short compact swing from the left side - he should be at Lakewood next summer.

Mickey Moniak and Adam Haseley each played sparingly. Moniak had a nice game against the Braves with a double and single. Haseley didn't do much regarding hits and looked a bit tired to me, but I think he just needs some time off during the offseason. He played a lot of games in college and the pros combined in 2017.

Yahir Gurrola, Julio Francisco and Simon Muzziotti all displayed speed and line drive bats. They appear to be in the Carlos Tocci mold. Can't teach speed, is a good thing to have.

Ben Pelletier reminds me of a young Pat Burrell. Big time pop in this teenager's bat. He didn't play much in FIL games, but I watch hands and bat speed and in the few at bats I saw he has a quick direct path through the ball.

Sixto Sanchez – Photo by Mark Wylie

Catcher Rodolfo Duran completes a double play by applying

tag on throw to home - Photo by Mark Wylie

Jose Jimenez

Chapter Twelve - Awards and Statistics

2017 Minor League Champions:

Triple-A:

International League - Durham (Rays) defeated Scranton/Wilkes-Barre (Yankees) 3 games to 1 in the Finals

Pacific Coast League - Memphis (Cardinals) defeated El Paso (Padres) 3 games to 2 in the Finals

Durham defeated Memphis 5-3 in the championship game to win the overall AAA crown.

Mexican League - Tijuana defeated Puebla 4 games to 1 in the Finals

Double-A:

Eastern League - Altoona (Pirates) defeated Trenton (Yankees) 3 games to 0 in the Finals

Southern League - Pensacola (Reds) and Chattanooga (Twins) declared Co-Champions - Finals were cancelled due to Hurricane Irma

Texas League - Midland (Athletics) defeated Tulsa (Dodgers) 3 games to 2 in the Finals

Class A-Advanced:

California League - Modesto (Mariners) defeated Lancaster (Rockies) 3 games to 0 in the Finals

Carolina League - Down East (Rangers) and Lynchburg (Indians) declared Co-Champions - Finals were cancelled due to Hurricane Irma

Florida State League - Dunedin (Blue Jays) and Palm Beach (Cardinals) declared Co-Champions - Finals were cancelled due to Hurricane Irma

Class A:

Midwest League - Quad Cities (Astros) defeated Fort Wayne (Padres) 3 games to 0 in the Finals

South Atlantic League - Greenville (Red Sox) defeated Kannapolis (White Sox) 3 games to 1 in the Finals

Class A Short Season:

New York Penn League - Hudson Valley (Rays) defeated Vermont (Athletics) 2 games to 0 in the Finals

Northwest League - Vancouver (Blue Jays) defeated Eugene (Cubs) 3 games to 1 in the Finals

Rookie League:

Pioneer League - Ogden (Dodgers) defeated Great Falls (White Sox) 2 games to 1 in the Finals

Appalachian League - Elizabethtown (Twins) defeated Pulaski (Yankees) 2 games to 0 in the Finals

Gulf Coast League - GCL Yankees East defeated GCL Nationals 2 games to 1 in the Finals

Arizona League - AZL Cubs defeated AZL Giants 2 games to 1 in the Finals

Dominican Summer League - DSL Dodgers2 defeated DSL Dodgers 6-4 in Championship Game

Championships by Organization:

Cardinals: 3
Dodgers: 3
Rays: 2
Twins: 2
Blue Jays: 2
Pirates: 1
Reds: 1
Mariners: 1
Rangers: 1
Indians: 1
Red Sox: 1
Yankees: 1
Cubs: 1
Athletics: 1
Astros: 1

Win-Loss Analysis - Minor League Systems

The Twins ended up with the best overall winning percentage of .592. The Phillies finish fifth best overall with a winning percentage of .531.

In reviewing just short season play (including the DSL) the Dodgers stood out and led with a .637 winning percentage, the Phillies were sixth best at .547.

In reviewing just full season play the Yankees led with a .611 winning percentage. The Phillies were tied for ninth at .522.

When reviewing just North America-based teams (excluding the DSL) the Yankees again lead with a .602 winning percentage bolstered by their full season clubs. The Phillies had the sixth best percentage at .528.

26 of the 30 systems had at least one playoff qualifier. The only four organizations that didn't have a playoff qualifier were the Angels, Braves, Giants and Nationals.

Regarding the systems with most playoff qualifiers, the Yankees led with seven playoff teams while the Dodgers and Twins had six each.

Phillies System - League Leaders:

International League - AAA:

- RBIs: Rhys Hoskins - 91
- Walks: JP Crawford - 79
- Strikeouts: Dylan Cozens - 194
- Slugging Percentage: Rhys Hoskins - .581
- OPS: Rhys Hoskins - .966

- Losses: Jake Thompson - tied for first - 14
- Saves: Pedro Beato - 33
- WHIP (minimum 0.8 IP/league game): Tom Eshelman - 0.94
- Games Finished: Pedro Beato - 48

Eastern League - AA

- Triples: Carlos Tocci - tied for first - 7

Florida State League - High A

- Total Bases - Wilson Garcia - 202

- Games: Seth McGarry - tied for first - 44 (31 with Bradenton, 13 with Clearwater)
- Shutouts: Harold Arauz - tied for first - 1
- Saves: Jeff Singer & Seth McGarry - tied for first - 19 (McGarry had 14 with Bradenton, 5 with Clearwater)
- Games Finished: Seth McGarry – 38

South Atlantic League - Class A
- Home Runs: Darick Hall - 27
- RBIs: Darick Hall - 96
- Total Bases: Darick Hall - 227
- Slugging Percentage: Darick Hall -.533
- OPS: Darick Hall - .872
- Wins: McKenzie Mills - 12 (with Hagerstown)
- Saves: Will Hibbs - 20

MVP Winners:
- Rhys Hoskins - International League
- Darick Hall - South Atlantic League

Following are the individual leaders in various categories for the 2017 full season Phillies Minor League squads:

Pitching :

Wins :
Tom Eshelman – 13 – Reading/Lehigh
McKenzie Mills – 12 – Hagerstown/Clearwater
Brandon Leibrandt – 11 – Reading/Lehigh
Jo Jo Romero – 10 – Lakewood/Clearwater
Tyler Viza – 10 – Reading
Alejandro Requena – 9 – Asheville/Lakewood
Cole Irvin – 9 – Clearwater/Reading
Jacob Waguespack – 9 – Clearwater/Reading/Lehigh
Jose Taveras – 9 – Clearwater/Reading/Lehigh
Nick Fanti – 9 – Lakewood
Pat Vendittte – 9 – Lehigh

Innings Pitched :

Jose Taveras – 154.1 – Clearwater/Reading/Lehigh
Cole Irvin – 151.1 – Clearwater/Reading
Tom Eshelman – 150 – Reading/Lehigh
Tyler Viza – 139.2 – Reading
Brandon Leibrandt – 136.2 – Reading/Lehigh
Jo Jo Romero – 129 – Lakewood/Clearwater
Alejandro Requena – 128 – Asheville/Lakewood
Franklyn Kilome – 127 – Clearwater/Reading
Ranger Suarez – 122.2 – Lakewood/Clearwater
Nick Fanti – 120.1 - Lakewood
McKenzie Mills – 120.1 – Hagerstown/Clearwater
Adonis Medina – 119.2 – Lakewood

Games :
Pedro Beato – 54 – Lehigh
Pat Venditte – 52 – Lehigh
Jeff Singer – 49 – Clearwater/Reading
JD Hammer – 48 – Asheville/Lancaster/Clearwater
Michael Mariot – 45 – Lehigh
Will Hibbs – 45 – Lakewood/Clearwater
Seth McGarry – 44 – Bradenton/Clearwater
Alexis Rivero – 43 – Reading/Lehigh
Luke Leftwich – 42 – Clearwater
Austin Davis – 42 – Clearwater/Reading
Trevor Bettencourt – 41 – Lakewood/Clearwater
Colton Murray – 41 – Reading/Lehigh
Cesar Ramos – 40 – Lehigh
Jesen Therrien – 39 – Reading/Lehigh

Games Started :
Tyler Viza – 26 – Reading
Jose Taveras – 25 – Clearwater/Reading/Lehigh
Brandon Leibrandt – 25 – Reading/Lehigh
Cole Irvin – 24 – Clearwater/Reading
Franklyn Kilome- 24 – Clearwater/Reading
Tom Eshelman – 23 – Reading/Lehigh
Jo Jo Romero – 23 – Lakewood/Clearwater
Ranger Suarez – 22 – Lakewood/Clearwater
Jake Thompson – 22 – Lehigh
Drew Anderson – 22 – Reading/Lehigh
Adonis Medina – 22 – Lakewood

Saves :

Pedro Beato – LH	33
Jeff Singer – CW/Reading	21
Will Hibbs – LKWD/CW	20
Seth McGarry – BR/CW	19
J.D. Hammer – ASH/LAN/CW	13
Trevor Bettencourt – LKWD/CW	10
Jesen Therrien – Reading/LH	9
Victor Arano – Reading/LH	9
Luke Leftwich – CW	8
Garrett Cleavinger – Bowie/Reading	4

Holds :

Player	Holds
Austin Davis – CW/Reading	12
Michael Mariot – LH	9
Yacksel Rios – Reading/LH	8
Jesen Therrien – Reading/LH	7
Ranfi Casimiro – CW/Reading/LH	7
Pat Venditte – LH	6
Tyler Gilbert – CW	6
Tom Windle – Reading	6
Hoby Milner – LH	6
Casey Fien – LH	6
Trevor Bettencourt – LKWD	5
J.D. Hammer – ASH/LAN/CW	4
Garrett Cleavinger – Bowie/Reading	4

Strikeouts :

Jose Taveras – CW/Reading/LH	140
McKenzie Mills – HAG/CW	134
Adonis Medina – LKWD	133
Ranger Suarez – LKWD/Reading	128
JoJo Romero -LKWD/CW	128
Nick Fanti – LKWD	121
Cole Irvin – CW/Reading	118
Jacob Waguespack – CW/Reading/LH	108
Brandon Leibrandt – Reading/LH	105
Bailey Falter – LKWD	105
Alejandro Requena – ASH/LKWD	104
Franklyn Kilome – CW/Reading	103
Tom Eshelman – Reading/LH	102
Tyler Viza – Reading	100

Games Finished :

Pedro Beato – LH	48
Jeff Singer – CW/Reading	39
Seth McGarry – BRD/CW	38
Will Hibbs – LKWD/CW	38
Trevor Bettencourt – LKWD/CW	27
J.D. Hammer – ASH/LAN/CW	26
Victor Arano – Reading/LH	23
Jesen Therrien – Reading/LH	20
Luke Leftwich – CW	20
Garrett Cleavinger – Bowie/Reading	17
Tyler Gilbert -CW	15
Colton Murray – Reading/LH	15
Jonathan Hennigan - LKWD	15
Miguel Nunez – Reading	15

ERA – Relievers (At Least 50 IP)

Jesen Therrien – Reading/LH	1.41
J.D. Hammer – ASH/LAN/CW	1.87
Yacksel Rios – Reading/LH	1.92
Harold Arauz – LKWD/CW/Reading	1.97
Seth McGarry – BRD/CW	2.32
Will Hibbs – LKWD/CW	2.51
Austin Davis – CW/Reading	2.60
Trevor Bettencourt – LKWD/CW	2.61
Joey DeNato – Reading/LH	2.65
Luke Leftwich – CW	2.70
Tyler Gilbert – CW	2.95
Jeff Singer – CW/Reading	3.00
Pedro Beato – LH	3.30

ERA – Starters (At Least 95 IP)

JoJo Romero – LKWD/CW	2.16
Jose Taveras – CW/Reading/LH	2.22
Ranger Suarez – LKWD/CW	2.27
Tom Eshelman – Reading/LH	2.40
Nick Fanti – LKWD	2.54
Alejandro Requena – ASH/LKWD	2.74
Franklyn Kilome – CW/Reading	2.83
Bailey Falter - LKWD	2.99
Adonis Medina – LKWD	3.01
Sixto Sanchez – LKWD/CW	3.03
Ben Lively – LH	3.15

WHIP – Relievers (At Least 50 IP)

Yacksel Rios – Reading/LH	0.82
Jesen Therrien – Reading/LH	0.84
Harold Arauz – LKWD/CW/Reading	0.88
J.D. Hammer – ASH/LAN/CW	0.88
Trevor Bettencourt – LKWD/CW	0.92
Will Hibbs – LKWD/CW	0.94
Seth McGarry – BRD/CW	0.99
Ranfi Casimiro – CW/Reading/LH	1.12
Luke Leftwich – CW	1.13
Tom Windle -Reading	1.14

WHIP – Starters (At Least 95 IP)

Name	WHIP
Nick Fanti – LKWD	0.96
Sixto Sanchez – LKWD/CW	0.96
Tom Eshelman – LH	0.97
McKenzie Mills – HAG/CW	1.00
Jose Taveras – CW/Reading/LH	1.04
Alejandro Requena – ASH/LKWD	1.05
Ranger Suarez – LKWD/CW	1.06
JoJo Romero – LKWD/CW	1.09
Drew Anderson – Reading/LH	1.12
Ben Lively – LH	1.16
Cole Irvin – CW/Reading	1.18
Adonis Medina – LKWD	1.19

Hitting :

Games Played :

Dylan Cozens – Lehigh	135
Andrew Pullin – Reading/Lehigh	134
Scott Kingery – Reading/Lehigh	132
Carlos Tocci – Reading/Lehigh	130
Zachary Coppola – Clearwater/Reading	130
J.P. Crawford – Lehigh	127
Jiandido Tromp – Reading/Lehigh	125
Kyle Martin – Reading	123
Mickey Moniak – Lakewood	123
Cornelius Randolph – Clearwater	122
Darick Hall – Lakewood/Clearwater	121
Wilson Garcia – Clearwater	121
Luke Williams – Lakewood	115
Rhys Hoskins – Lehigh	115
Luke Williams – Lehigh	115

At Bats

Scott Kingery – Reading/Lehigh	543
Andrew Pullin – Reading/Lehigh	504
Zachary Coppola – CW/Reading	485
Carlos Tocci – Reading/Lehigh	483
Wilson Garcia – Clearwater	477
Dylan Cozens – Lehigh	476
J.P. Crawford – Lehigh	474
Mickey Moniak – Lakewood	466
Jiandido Tromp – Reading/LH	465
Darick Hall – Lakewood/CW	452
Daniel Brito – Lakewood	447
Cornelius Randolph – Clearwater	440
Kyle Martin – Reading	436
Jose Gomez – Asheville/CW	416
Mark Laird – Clearwater	406

Runs Scored

Scott Kingery – Reading/LH	103
Rhys Hoskins – Lehigh	78
J.P. Crawford – Lehigh	75
Zachary Coppola – CW/Reading	69
Dylan Cozens – Lehigh	68
Darick Hall – Lakewood/CW	68
Jiandido Tromp – Reading/LH	64
Jose Gomez – Asheville/CW	63
Andrew Pullin – Reading/LH	62
Carlos Tocci – Reading/LH	61
Kyle Martin – Reading	60
Mark Laird – Clearwater	56
Daniel Brito – Lakewood	54
Angelo Mora – Reading/LH	54
Mickey Moniak – Lakewood	53

Hits

Scott Kingery – Reading/LH	165
Carlos Tocci – Reading/LH	142
Zachary Coppola – CW/Reading	138
Andrew Pullin – Reading/LH	137
Jiandido Tromp – Reading/LH	132
Wilson Garcia – Clearwater	131
Jose Gomez – Asheville/CW	129
Darick Hall – Lakewood/CW	122
Mark Laird – Clearwater	116
Angelo Mora – Reading/LH	116
J.P. Crawford – Lehigh	115
Rhys Hoskins – Lehigh	114
Damek Tomscha – CW/Reading	111
Mickey Moniak – Lakewood	110
Cornelius Randolph – Clearwater	110

Doubles

Andrew Pullin – Reading/Lehigh	43
Jiandido Tromp – Reading/Lehigh	32
Darick Hall – Lakewood/Clearwater	30
Scott Kingery – Reading/Lehigh	29
Wilson Garcia – Clearwater	28
Cord Sandberg – LKWD/CW/Reading	28
Rhys Hoskins – Lehigh	24
Angelo Mora – Reading/Lehigh	24
Henri Lartigue – Lakewood	23
Mickey Moniak – Lakewood	22
Malquin Canelo – Reading	22
Jose Gomez – Asheville/Clearwater	22
J.P. Crawford – Lehigh	20
Carlos Tocci – Reading/Lehigh	19
Cornelius Randolph – Clearwater	18
Cameron Perkins – Lehigh	18

Triples

Scott Kingery – Reading/Lehigh	8
Carlos Tocci – Reading/Lehigh	7
Mickey Moniak – Lakewood	6
J.P. Crawford – Lehigh	6
Cornelius Randolph – Clearwater	5
Mark Laird – Clearwater	5
Rhys Hoskins – Lehigh	4
Henri Lartigue – Lakewood	4
Emmanuel Marrero – Clearwater	4
Mitch Walding – Reading	4
Carlos Duran – Lakewood/CW	4
Andrew Pullin – Reading/Lehigh	3
Jiandido Tromp – Reading/Lehigh	3
Angelo Mora – Reading/Lehigh	3
Dylan Cozens – Lehigh	3
Arquimedes Gamboa – Lakewood	3
Jan Hernandez – Clearwater	3
Roman Quinn – Lehigh	3

Home Runs

Rhys Hoskins – Lehigh	29
Darick Hall – LKWD/CW	29
Dylan Cozens – Lehigh	27
Scott Kingery – Reading/LH	26
Mitch Walding – Reading	25
Kyle Martin – Reading	22
Andrew Pullin – Reading/LH	20
Jiandido Tromp – Reading/LH	18
Jan Hernandez – Clearwater	16
J.P. Crawford – Lehigh	15
Nick Williams – Lehigh	15
Cornelius Randolph – Clearwater	13
Wilson Garcia – Clearwater	13
Deivi Grullon – CW/Reading	12
Herlis Rodriguez – CW/Reading/LH	11
Damek Tomscha – CW/Reading	11

RBI's

Darick Hall – Lakewood/CW	101
Rhys Hoskins – Lehigh	91
Dylan Cozens – Lehigh	75
Andrew Pullin – Reading/LH	69
Kyle Martin – Reading	68
Scott Kingery – Reading/LH	65
Jiandido Tromp – Reading/LH	64
J.P. Crawford – Lehigh	63
Mitch Walding – Reading	62
Wilson Garcia – Clearwater	60
Cornelius Randolph – CW	55
Angelo Mora – Reading/LH	55
Carlos Tocci – Reading/LH	52
Damek Tomscha – CW/Reading	50
Nick Williams – Lehigh	44
Henri Lartigue – Lakewood	44
Mickey Moniak – Lakewood	44

Total Bases

Scott Kingery – Reading/Lehigh	288
Andrew Pullin – Reading/Lehigh	246
Darick Hall – Lakewood/Clearwater	241
Rhys Hoskins – Lehigh	233
Jiandido Tromp – Reading/Lehigh	224
Wilson Garcia – Clearwater	202
Dylan Cozens – Lehigh	199
J.P. Crawford – Lehigh	192
Carlos Tocci – Reading/Lehigh	184
Mitch Walding -Reading	181
Cornelius Randolph – Clearwater	177
Angelo Mora – Reading/Lehigh	173
Kyle Martin – Reading	167
Jose Gomez – Asheville/Clearwater	167
Damek Tomscha – CW/Reading	159
Mickey Moniak – Lakewood	159
Zachary Coppola – CW/Reading	159

Walks

J.P. Crawford – Lehigh	79
Rhys Hoskins – Lehigh	64
Dylan Cozens – Lehigh	58
Cornelius Randolph – Clearwater	55
Zachary Coppola – Clearwater/Reading	55
Kyle Martin – Reading	50
Mitch Walding – Reading	44
Malquin Canelo – Reading	42
Scott Kingery – Reading/Lehigh	41
Drew Stankiewicz – CW/Reading	41
Damek Tomscha – CW/Reading	38
Andrew Pullin – Reading/Lehigh	35
Pedro Florimon – Lehigh	34
Daniel Brito – Lakewood	33
Arquimedes Gamboa – Lakewood	33

Strikeouts

Dylan Cozens – Lehigh	194
Jose Pujols – Clearwater	150
Kyle Martin – Reading	134
Mitch Walding – Reading	127
Cornelius Randolph – CW	125
Darick Hall – Lakewood/CW	117
Jiandido Tromp – Reading/LH	114
Jan Hernandez – Clearwater	114
Malquin Canelo – Reading	113
Jorge Alfaro – Lehigh	113
Scott Kingery – Reading/LH	109
Mickey Moniak – Lakewood	109
Cord Sandberg – LKWD/CW/Reading	103
J.P. Crawford – Lehigh	97
Daniel Brito – Lakewood	95

Stolen Bases

Zachary Coppola – CW/Reading	39
Scott Kingery – Reading/LH	29
Luke Williams – Lakewood	29
Jose Gomez – Asheville/CW	18
Grenny Cumana – Clearwater	16
Malquin Canelo – Reading	12
Daniel Brito – Lakewood	12
Mickey Moniak – Lakewood	11
Emmanuel Marrero -Clearwater	11
Carlos Duran – LKWD/CW	11
Mark Laird – Clearwater	11
Jiandido Tromp – Reading/LH	10
Herlis Rodriguez – CW/Reading/LH	10
Raul Rivas – Lakewood	10
Roman Quinn – Lehigh	10

On Base Pct (at least 300 AB's)	OBP	AB's
Damek Tomscha – CW/Reading	0.386	360
Rhys Hoskins – Lehigh	0.385	401
Drew Stankiewicz – CW/Reading	0.364	328
Scott Kingery – Reading/Lehigh	0.359	543
Zachary Coppola – CW/Reading	0.357	485
Jose Gomez – Asheville/CW	0.357	416
J.P. Crawford – Lehigh	0.351	474
Pedro Florimon – Lehigh	0.347	310
Carlos Tocci – Reading/LH	0.346	483
Mark Laird – Clearwater	0.338	406
Cornelius Randolph – Clearwater	0.338	440
Angelo Mora – Reading/LH	0.334	398
Darick Hall – Lakewood/CW	0.334	452
Edgar Cabral – Lakewood/CW	0.332	319
Jiandido Tromp – Reading/LH	0.328	465
Arquimedes Gamboa – Lakewood	0.328	307
Andrew Pullin – Reading/LH	0.327	504
Mitch Walding – Reading	0.327	351

Slugging Pct (at least 300 AB's)	SLG	AB's
Rhys Hoskins – Lehigh	0.581	401
Darick Hall – Lakewood/CW	0.533	452
Scott Kingery -Reading/Lehigh	0.530	543
Mitch Walding – Reading	0.516	351
Nick Williams – Lehigh	0.511	282
Andrew Pullin – Reading/Lehigh	0.488	504
Jiandido Tromp – Reading/Lehigh	0.482	465
Damek Tomscha -CW/Reading	0.439	360
Angelo Mora – Reading/Lehigh	0.435	398
Cord Sandberg – LKWD/CW/Reading	0.431	362
Wilson Garcia – Clearwater	0.423	477
Drew Stankiewicz – CW/Reading	0.421	328
Dylan Cozens – Lehigh	0.418	476
Jan Hernandez – Clearwater	0.415	316
Pedro Florimon – Lehigh	0.410	310
Henri Lartigue – Lakewood	0.410	339
J.P. Crawford – Lehigh	0.405	474

Batting Average (at least 300 AB's)	AVG	AB's
Jose Gomez – Asheville/Clearwater	0.310	416
Damek Tomscha – CW/Reading	0.307	360
Scott Kingery – Reading/Lehigh	0.304	543
Carlos Tocci – Reading/Lehigh	0.294	483
Angelo Mora – Reading/Lehigh	0.291	398
Mark Laird – Clearwater	0.286	406
Zachary Coppola – CW/Reading	0.285	485
Rhys Hoskins – Lehigh	0.284	401
Jiandido Tromp – Reading/Lehigh	0.284	465
Drew Stankiewicz – CW/Reading	0.280	328
Wilson Garcia – Clearwater	0.275	477
Andrew Pullin – Reading/Lehigh	0.272	504
Darick Hall – Lakewood/Clearwater	0.270	452
Cord Sandberg – LKWD/CW/Reading	0.268	362
Pedro Florimon – Lehigh	0.265	310
Arquimedes Gamboa – Lakewood	0.261	307
Edgar Cabral – LKWD/Clearwater	0.260	319

OPS (at least 300 AB's)	OPS	AB's
Rhys Hoskins – Lehigh	0.966	401
Scott Kingery – Reading/Lehigh	0.889	543
Darick Hall – Lakewood/Clearwater	0.867	452
Mitch Walding – Reading	0.842	351
Damek Tomscha – CW/Reading	0.825	360
Andrew Pullin – Reading/Lehigh	0.815	504
Jiandido Tromp – Reading/Lehigh	0.810	465
Drew Stankiewicz – CW/Reading	0.784	328
Angelo Mora – Reading/Lehigh	0.765	398
Jose Gomez – Asheville/Clearwater	0.759	416
Pedro Florimon – Lehigh	0.756	310
J.P. Crawford – Lehigh	0.756	474
Cord Sandberg – LKWD/CW/Reading	0.740	362
Cornelius Randolph – Clearwater	0.740	440
Carlos Tocci – Reading/Lehigh	0.727	483
Wilson Garcia – Clearwater	0.721	477
Dylan Cozens – Lehigh	0.719	476
Herlis Rodriguez – CW/Reading/LH	0.712	357

Following are the individual leaders in various categories for the 2017 short season Phillies Minor League squads :

Hitting :

Games Played		
Alexito Feliz	DSL Phillies White	69
Nicolas Torres	DSL Phillies White	69
Julio Francisco	DSL Phillies White	68
Jose Tortolero	DSL Phillies White	67
Raymond Mora	DSL Phillies White	67
Carlos Oropeza	DSL Phillies Red	64
Josh Stephen	Williamsport	64
Greg Pickett	Williamsport	62
Jake Scheiner	Williamsport	61
Jevi Hernandez	DSL Phillies Red	61
Luis Matos	DSL Phillies Red	60
Yahir Gurrola	GCL/Williamsport	60
Yerwin Trejo	DSL Phillies White	59
Christian Valerio	DSL Phillies Red	58
Nick Maton	Williamsport	58

At Bats		
Alexito Feliz	DSL Phillies White	247
Julio Francisco	DSL Phillies White	242
Nicolas Torres	DSL Phillies White	240
Josh Stephen	Williamsport	239
Jake Scheiner	Williamsport	236
Greg Pickett	Williamsport	221
Jose Tortolero	DSL Phillies White	218
Carlos Oropeza	DSL Phillies Red	218
Raymond Mora	DSL Phillies White	211
Jevi Hernandez	DSL Phillies Red	211
Nick Maton	Williamsport	210
Luis Rojas	DSL Phillies Red	207
Christian Valerio	DSL Phillies Red	206
Yahir Gurrola	GCL/Williamsport	202
Cole Stobbe	Williamsport	197

Runs		
Julio Francisco	DSL Phillies White	51
Nicolas Torres	DSL Phillies White	40
Nick Maton	Williamsport	34
Alexito Feliz	DSL Phillies White	33
Jake Scheiner	Williamsport	32
Kevin Markham	GCL Phillies	32
Yahir Gurrola	GCL/Williamsport	31
Yerwin Trejo	DSL Phillies White	29
Edgar Made	DSL Phillies Red	29
Jose Tortolero	DSL Phillies White	28
Christian Valerio	DSL Phillies Red	28
Cole Stobbe	Williamsport	28
Luis Matos	DSL Phillies Red	28
Raymond Mora	DSL Phillies White	27
Luis Rojas	DSL Phillies Red	27

Hits		
Nicolas Torres	DSL Phillies White	80
Julio Francisco	DSL Phillies White	77
Alexito Feliz	DSL Phillies White	73
Greg Pickett	Williamsport	60
Jake Scheiner	Williamsport	59
Josh Stephen	Williamsport	59
Carlos Oropeza	DSL Phillies Red	59
Yahir Gurrola	GCL/Williamsport	58
Ben Pelletier	GCL Phillies	57
Luis Rojas	DSL Phillies Red	54
Nick Maton	Williamsport	53
Juan Mendez	DSL Phillies White	53
Yerwin Trejo	DSL Phillies White	52
Christian Valerio	DSL Phillies Red	51
Raymond Mora	DSL Phillies White	51

Doubles		
Jevi Hernandez	DSL Phillies Red	16
Jhailyn Ortiz	Williamsport	15
Malvin Matos	Williamsport	15
Jake Scheiner	Williamsport	14
Nicolas Torres	DSL Phillies White	13
Yahir Gurrola	GCL/Williamsport	13
Ben Pelletier	GCL Phillies	13
Quincy Nieporte	GCL Phillies	13
Maximo De La Rosa	DSL Phillies Red	13
Carlos Oropeza	DSL Phillies Red	12
Josh Stephen	Williamsport	12

Triples		
Julio Francisco	DSL Phillies White	10
Juan Mendez	DSL Phillies White	7
Simon Muzziotti	GCL Phillies	6
Josh Stephen	Williamsport	5
Edgar Made	DSL Phillies Red	5
Nicolas Torres	DSL Phillies White	4
Jevi Hernandez	DSL Phillies Red	3
Alexito Feliz	DSL Phillies White	3
Jose Tortolero	DSL Phillies White	3
Rodolfo Duran	Williamsport	3
Luis Rojas	DSL Phillies Red	3
Yerwin Trejo	DSL Phillies White	3
Wilbert Garcia	DSL Phillies Red	3

Home Runs		
Jhailyn Ortiz	Williamsport	8
Cole Stobbe	Williamsport	8
Greg Pickett	Williamsport	6
Quincy Nieporte	GCL Phillies	5
Alexito Feliz	DSL Phillies White	4
Jake Scheiner	Williamsport	4
Juan Mendez	DSL Phillies White	3
Malvin Matos	Williamsport	3
Ben Pelletier	GCL Phillies	3
Austin Listi	Williamsport	3
Edwin Rodriguez	GCL Phillies	3
Zach Green	GCL Phillies	3

RBI's		
Quincy Nieporte	GCL Phillies	35
Alexito Feliz	DSL Phillies White	35
Jevi Hernandez	DSL Phillies Red	31
Jhailyn Ortiz	Williamsport	30
Carlos Oropeza	DSL Phillies Red	30
Yahir Gurrola	GCL/Williamsport	30
Josh Stephen	Williamsport	28
Nicolas Torres	DSL Phillies White	28
Luis Rojas	DSL Phillies Red	27
Juan Mendez	DSL Phillies White	26
Ben Pelletier	GCL Phillies	26
Greg Pickett	Williamsport	25
Brayan Gonzalez	GCL Phillies	24
Cole Stobbe	Williamsport	22
Adam Haseley	GCL/Williamsport	22

Total Bases		
Julio Francisco	DSL Phillies White	107
Alexito Feliz	DSL Phillies White	101
Nicolas Torres	DSL Phillies White	101
Jhailyn Ortiz	Williamsport	89
Greg Pickett	Williamsport	89
Jake Scheiner	Williamsport	89
Josh Stephen	Williamsport	87
Ben Pelletier	GCL Phillies	81
Juan Mendez	DSL Phillies White	80
Carlos Oropeza	DSL Phillies Red	78
Quincy Nieporte	GCL Phillies	76
Jevi Hernandez	DSL Phillies Red	74
Yahir Gurrola	GCL/Williamsport	74
Cole Stobbe	Williamsport	74
Malvin Matos	Williamsport	71

Walks		
Nick Maton	Williamsport	30
Julio Francisco	DSL Phillies White	28
Yerwin Trejo	DSL Phillies White	27
Christian Valerio	DSL Phillies Red	26
Greg Pickett	Williamsport	25
Edgar Made	DSL Phillies Red	25
Luis Matos	DSL Phillies Red	23
Kevin Markham	GCL Phillies	22
Jose Tortolero	DSL Phillies White	21
Jose Rivera	DSL Phillies Red	21
Carlos Oropeza	DSL Phillies Red	20
Malvin Matos	Williamsport	20
Raymond Mora	DSL Phillies White	20
Jhailyn Ortiz	Williamsport	18
Keudy Bocio	GCL Phillies	18
Cole Stobbe	Williamsport	17
Dixon Gutierrez	DSL Phillies Red	17

Strikeouts		
Greg Pickett	Williamsport	70
Cole Stobbe	Williamsport	67
Jake Scheiner	Williamsport	54
Raymond Mora	DSL Phillies White	52
Josh Stephen	Williamsport	50
Luis Matos	DSL Phillies Red	48
Nick Maton	Williamsport	47
Jhailyn Ortiz	Williamsport	47
Yahir Gurrola	GCL/Williamsport	42
Brian Mims	Williamsport	42
Jose Tortolero	DSL Phillies White	40
Christian Valerio	DSL Phillies Red	39
Malvin Matos	Williamsport	39
Luiggi Mujica	DSL Phillies Red	39
Juan Herrera	DSL Phillies White	37

Stolen Bases		
Julio Francisco	DSL Phillies White	22
Yerwin Trejo	DSL Phillies White	21
Alexito Feliz	DSL Phillies White	20
Luis Matos	DSL Phillies Red	15
Yahir Gurrola	GCL/Williamsport	15
Christian Valerio	DSL Phillies Red	14
Edgar Made	DSL Phillies Red	14
Luis Rojas	DSL Phillies Red	14
Jose Tortolero	DSL Phillies White	12
Jevi Hernandez	DSL Phillies Red	11
Nicolas Torres	DSL Phillies White	11
Nick Maton	Williamsport	10
Wilbert Garcia	DSL Phillies Red	10
Luiggi Mujica	DSL Phillies Red	9
Dixon Gutierrez	DSL Phillies Red	9

OBP - Minimum 75 At Bats			AB's
Jose Rivera	DSL Phillies Red	0.432	102
Juan Mendez	DSL Phillies White	0.411	140
Jhailyn Ortiz	Williamsport	0.401	159
Julio Francisco	DSL Phillies White	0.399	242
Nicolas Torres	DSL Phillies White	0.383	240
Yerwin Trejo	DSL Phillies White	0.381	191
Keudy Bocio	GCL Phillies	0.374	115
Austin Listi	Williamsport	0.372	75
Jonathan Guzman	GCL/Williamsport	0.370	172
Kevin Markham	GCL Phillies	0.369	140
Adam Haseley	GCL/Williamsport	0.364	149
Ben Pelletier	GCL Phillies	0.361	171
Quincy Nieporte	GCL Phillies	0.355	154
Yahir Gurrola	GCL/Williamsport	0.354	202
Nick Maton	Williamsport	0.350	210

Slugging Pct - Minimum 75 At Bats			AB's
Juan Mendez	DSL Phillies White	0.571	140
Jhailyn Ortiz	Williamsport	0.560	159
Adam Haseley	GCL/Williamsport	0.503	149
Quincy Nieporte	GCL Phillies	0.494	154
Austin Listi	Williamsport	0.480	75
Ben Pelletier	GCL Phillies	0.474	171
Julio Francisco	DSL Phillies White	0.442	242
Nicolas Torres	DSL Phillies White	0.421	240
Alexito Feliz	DSL Phillies White	0.409	247
Greg Pickett	Williamsport	0.403	221
Malvin Matos	Williamsport	0.401	177
Danny Mayer	GCL Phillies	0.396	106
Brayan Gonzalez	GCL Phillies	0.388	134
Simon Muzziotti	GCL Phillies	0.388	134

Batting Average - Minimum 75 At Bats			AB's
Juan Mendez	DSL Phillies White	0.379	140
Ben Pelletier	GCL Phillies	0.333	171
Nicolas Torres	DSL Phillies White	0.333	240
Julio Francisco	DSL Phillies White	0.318	242
Jhailyn Ortiz	Williamsport	0.302	159
Jonathan Guzman	GCL/Williamsport	0.300	172
Quincy Nieporte	GCL Phillies	0.299	154
Alexito Feliz	DSL Phillies White	0.296	247
Adam Haseley	GCL/Williamsport	0.295	149
Austin Listi	Williamsport	0.293	75
Yahir Gurrola	GCL/Williamsport	0.287	202
Jose Rivera	DSL Phillies Red	0.284	102
Keudy Bocio	GCL Phillies	0.278	115
Yerwin Trejo	DSL Phillies White	0.272	191
Greg Pickett	Williamsport	0.271	221
Carlos Oropeza	DSL Phillies Red	0.271	218
Brayan Gonzalez	GCL Phillies	0.269	134
Simon Muzziotti	GCL Phillies	0.269	134

OPS - Minimum 75 At Bats			AB's
Juan Mendez	DSL Phillies White	0.982	140
Jhailyn Ortiz	Williamsport	0.961	159
Adam Haseley	GCL/Williamsport	0.867	149
Austin Listi	Williamsport	0.852	75
Quincy Nieporte	GCL Phillies	0.848	154
Julio Francisco	DSL Phillies White	0.841	242
Ben Pelletier	GCL Phillies	0.835	171
Nicolas Torres	DSL Phillies White	0.804	240
Jose Rivera	DSL Phillies Red	0.765	102
Malvin Matos	Williamsport	0.747	177
Greg Pickett	Williamsport	0.745	221
Alexito Feliz	DSL Phillies White	0.742	247
Danny Mayer	GCL Phillies	0.738	106
Yerwin Trejo	DSL Phillies White	0.731	191
Kevin Markham	GCL Phillies	0.726	140

Pitching :

Wins		
Kyle Young	Williamsport Cross Cutters	7
Leonel Aponte	DSL Phillies Red	7
Ramon Rosso	DSL Phillies White/GCL/Williamsport	7
Bryan Alcala	DSL Phillies White	6
Ludovico Coveri	DSL Phillies Red	6
Manuel Silva	GCL Phillies	6
Jonas De La Cruz	DSL Phillies White	5
Roimy Mendoza	DSL Phillies Red	5
Anderson Parra	DSL Phillies White	4
Andrew Brown	Williamsport Cross Cutters	4
Carlos Salazar	DSL Phillies White	4
Julian Garcia	Williamsport Cross Cutters	4
Oscar Marcelino	GCL Phillies	4
Victor Santos	DSL Phillies Red	4
Will Stewart	Williamsport Cross Cutters	4

Games		
Ludovico Coveri	DSL Phillies Red	24
Abdallah Aris	DSL Phillies Red	23
Luis Ramirez	Williamsport Cross Cutters	23
Moises Nolasco	DSL Phillies Red	23
Wilberson Liendo	DSL Phillies Red	19
Carlos Salazar	DSL Phillies White	19
Randy Alcantara	Williamsport Cross Cutters	19
Roimy Mendoza	DSL Phillies Red	19
Eudiver Avendano	DSL Phillies Red	18
Oscar Marcelino	GCL Phillies	17
Tyler Frohwirth	Williamsport Cross Cutters	17
Connor Brogdon	Williamsport Cross Cutters	16
Alfredo Benitez	DSL Phillies White	16
Zach Warren	Williamsport Cross Cutters	16
Jhon Nunez	Williamsport Cross Cutters	16

Starts		
Ramon Rosso	DSL Phillies White/GCL/Williamsport	14
Jonas De La Cruz	DSL Phillies White	14
Juan Santos	DSL Phillies Red	14
Leonel Aponte	DSL Phillies Red	13
Bryan Alcala	DSL Phillies White	13
Antonio Canizales	DSL Phillies Red	13
Kyle Young	Williamsport Cross Cutters	13
Julian Garcia	Williamsport Cross Cutters	13
Will Stewart	Williamsport Cross Cutters	13
Erick Heredia	DSL Phillies Red	12
Carlos Francisco	DSL Phillies White	11
Andrew Brown	Williamsport Cross Cutters	10
Victor Santos	DSL Phillies Red	9
Francisco Morales	GCL Phillies	9
Jhordany Mezquita	GCL Phillies	9
Manuel Silva	GCL Phillies	9
Spencer Howard	Williamsport Cross Cutters	9

Saves		
Luis Ramirez	Williamsport Cross Cutters	11
Abdallah Aris	DSL Phillies Red	8
Carlos Salazar	DSL Phillies White	6
Ludovico Coveri	DSL Phillies Red	5
Anton Kuznetsov	GCL Phillies	5
Randy Alcantara	Williamsport Cross Cutters	5
Yorbys Tabares	DSL Phillies White	5
Moises Nolasco	DSL Phillies Red	4
Jose Perez	DSL Phillies White	3
Connor Brogdon	Williamsport Cross Cutters	3
Damon Jones	Williamsport Cross Cutters	3
Oscar Marcelino	GCL Phillies	2
Alfredo Benitez	DSL Phillies White	2
Yeison Sanchez	DSL Phillies White	2
Alexis Herrera	DSL Phillies White	2

Innings Pitched		
Leonel Aponte	DSL Phillies Red	81.1
Ramon Rosso	DSL Phillies White/GCL/Williamsport	75.2
Bryan Alcala	DSL Phillies White	67
Antonio Canizales	DSL Phillies Red	65.1
Kyle Young	Williamsport Cross Cutters	65
Andrew Brown	Williamsport Cross Cutters	63.2
Jonas De La Cruz	DSL Phillies White	63
Juan Santos	DSL Phillies Red	61
Will Stewart	Williamsport Cross Cutters	60.1
Julian Garcia	Williamsport Cross Cutters	60
Ludovico Coveri	DSL Phillies Red	53.2
Carlos Francisco	DSL Phillies White	50
Erick Heredia	DSL Phillies Red	49
Victor Santos	DSL Phillies Red	49
Sandro Rosario	GCL Phillies	49

Strikeouts		
Ramon Rosso	DSL Phillies White/GCL/Williamsport	105
Julian Garcia	Williamsport Cross Cutters	82
Kyle Young	Williamsport Cross Cutters	72
Leonel Aponte	DSL Phillies Red	69
Jonas De La Cruz	DSL Phillies White	60
Will Stewart	Williamsport Cross Cutters	58
Bryan Alcala	DSL Phillies White	53
Abdallah Aris	DSL Phillies Red	51
Antonio Canizales	DSL Phillies Red	48
Andrew Brown	Williamsport Cross Cutters	47
Eudiver Avendano	DSL Phillies Red	46
Connor Brogdon	Williamsport Cross Cutters	45
Juan Santos	DSL Phillies Red	44
Francisco Morales	GCL Phillies	44
Wilberson Liendo	DSL Phillies Red	43
David Parkinson	Williamsport Cross Cutters	42

Holds		
Randy Alcantara	Williamsport Cross Cutters	4
Eudiver Avendano	DSL Phillies Red	3
Connor Brogdon	Williamsport Cross Cutters	3
David Parkinson	Williamsport Cross Cutters	3
Santy Prada	DSL Phillies White	3
Junior Tejada	DSL Phillies Red	3
Zach Warren	Williamsport Cross Cutters	2
Moises Nolasco	DSL Phillies Red	2
Aldemar Rivas	DSL Phillies White	2
Roimy Mendoza	DSL Phillies Red	2
Ramiro Soto	DSL Phillies White	2
Orestes Melendez	Williamsport Cross Cutters	2
Anderson Parra	DSL Phillies White	2
Oscar Marcelino	GCL Phillies	2
Kyle Dohy	Williamsport Cross Cutters	2
Ben Brown	GCL Phillies	2
Jake Kelzer	Williamsport Cross Cutters	2

WHIP (At Least 25 IP)			IP
Anton Kuznetsov	GCL Phillies	0.79	25.1
Leonel Aponte	DSL Phillies Red	0.79	81.1
Jhordany Mezquita	GCL Phillies	0.85	37.2
Ramon Rosso	DSL Phillies White/GCL/Williamsport	1.02	75.2
Ludovico Coveri	DSL Phillies Red	1.02	53.2
Carlos Salazar	DSL Phillies White	1.02	46
Aldemar Rivas	DSL Phillies White	1.02	31.1
Oscar Marcelino	GCL Phillies	1.04	28
Randy Alcantara	Williamsport Cross Cutters	1.08	44.1
Jose Conopoima	DSL Phillies Red	1.10	35.1
Bryan Alcala	DSL Phillies White	1.12	67
Kyle Young	Williamsport Cross Cutters	1.12	65
Antonio Canizales	DSL Phillies Red	1.13	65.1
Connor Brogdon	Williamsport Cross Cutters	1.15	34.2
Victor Santos	DSL Phillies Red	1.16	49
Andrew Brown	Williamsport Cross Cutters	1.18	63.2

2017 PAUL OWENS AWARD WINNERS

SCOTT KINGERY

TOM ESHELMAN

Each year the best pitcher and position player in the Phillies system are awarded the Paul Owens Award. The 2017 Award Winners were Scott Kingery and Tom Eshelman

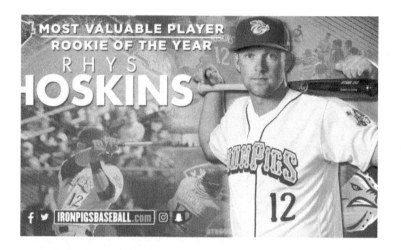

Rhys Hoskins was named the International League MVP and
Rookie of the Year

Darick Hall was named the South Atlantic League MVP

Every year the Phillies honor a player from each of their affiliates for community service. This year's award winners are pictured above with Joe Jordan, the Phillies Minor League Player Development Director, and Rhys Hoskins, who was an award winner in 2016. The winners were:

- Kyle Young – Williamsport
- Will Hibbs – Lakewood
- Luke Leftwich- Clearwater
- Michael Mariot – Lehigh Valley
- Cole Irvin – Reading

Chapter Thirteen - Player Prospectus – by position

In this chapter I'll do a position-by-position review of both the big club and the minor leagues as the team moves forward. This review was written in early December of 2017, and as such some of the players mentioned may have subsequently moved on from the organization.

Here's a look at First Base:

The Big Club:

Rhys Hoskins did things that no one else had even thought about doing in his brief major league career to date. Baseball seasons are marathons though, and not sprints, and there is no way the young man can keep up that pace. However, I've been touting his ability since we first saw him in his initial minor league camp. He's disciplined, smart and talented and has always in my opinion been capable of having a very special big league career. I see a favorable comparison to Paul Goldschmidt as he has that kind of talent and approach. First base is a position the club shouldn't have to worry about for at least 10 years. Mr. Hoskins is going get paid, and deservedly so.

Tommy Joseph put up numbers this season that would be very acceptable for a catcher. The thing is, he plays first base now. He hit 22 homers with 69 RBIs but posted a low slash line of .240/.289/.432 in 533 at bats. He's by all accounts a very good person and an excellent teammate, evident by shots of him in the dugout showing him pulling for his team. If the National League had the DH then Tommy would be a great candidate for the position. It's likely he is shopped this offseason, as he is only 26 and has a lot of baseball ahead of him, it's just a matter of where.

The Minors:

Brock Stassi was the ultimate feel good story when he made the big club out of spring training. The 28-year-old had a tough role as a bench player with limited at bats and rode the shuttle between the bigs and the minors a few times this summer before ultimately being removed from the 40-man roster and being designated for assignment, which he accepted to finish the year at Lehigh Valley. He hit .249/.325/.349 in 179 minor league at bats to complete the season. Brock signed with the Minnesota Twins on December 7th as a minor league free agent.

Kyle Martin had a rough year statistically, slashing .193/.288/.383 at Reading in 436 at bats, although he did pop 22 home runs and post 68 RBIs. He also struck out 134 times (31 percent) while walking 50 times. He was the Phillies fourth round selection in the 2015 draft out of the University of South Carolina and will turn 25 this November. Ideally, he should play at Lehigh Valley next summer and will spend this offseason in the Colombian Winter League working towards making a good impression in spring training and securing that spot.

Zach Green had an injury depleted year as he worked his way back from Tommy John surgery. He only amassed 198 at bats this summer between GCL/Clearwater/Reading and hit .227/.291/.424 with nine homers and 26 RBIs. Zach has been in the organization for six years now after being the club's third round pick in 2012, and yet is still just 23. He was chosen as a third baseman but has spent a good deal of his on-field time at first base. He's just never stayed healthy enough to put up solid numbers and has never had a season where he had more than 400 at bats. The closest he came was when he had 354 in 2016 with Clearwater. When you watch him in the cage he's got a level and quick swing and the ball flies off his bat. This true potential is the main reason why he's still around. I'd expect him to return to Reading this year, perhaps as the designated starter at third base.

Harold Martinez and his family are truly nice folks which has always made me pull for him. Harold is now 27 and has completed his seventh year of pro ball after being the Phillies' second round pick out of the University of Miami in 2011. He once again was a part-time player this summer, splitting time between Reading and Lehigh Valley and getting only 128 at bats as he also did a couple stints on the disabled list. He's going to test minor league free agency this offseason and likely lands with another organization.

Wilson Garcia is only 23 years old but has just completed his seventh pro season, and is therefore eligible for minor league free agency. He's been very steady in his career with a .283/.316/.379 career slash line in 1,667 at bats. He hit a solid .275/.298/.423 last summer for Clearwater in 477 at bats with 13 homers and 60 RBIs. If he stays with the Phillies he very likely is assigned to Reading in the same DH/1B role.

Darick Hall had a breakout year in 2017 winning the South Atlantic League MVP Award. The 22-year-old 16th round pick of the 2016 draft hit .270/.334/.533 with 29 home runs and 101 RBIs primarily at Lakewood but including a late-season callup to Clearwater where he played in seven games and got 26 at bats. I'm a big fan of his, as I see the same promise in him that I've seen previously in guys like Hoskins and Cozens.

Darick has pure power but he's not limited to just hitting the long ball, hitting 30 doubles this season. I believe he's going to be a productive big leaguer and isn't that far away from being so. The ideal plan would be that he has a decent spring training and gets assigned to Reading to begin next season, and at the least gets an assignment to Clearwater with a goal of an in-season promotion. This young man is one to watch; he may have to convert to the outfield to play alongside Hoskins, but he's athletic enough to do that also.

Twenty-three-year-old Austin Listi can play both outfield and first base. He began last season at Williamsport and finished up at Lakewood. Austin was the team's 17th round selection from the 2017 draft out of Dallas Baptist University. He slashed .262/.315/.451 in 195 at bats with 7 homers and 28 RBIs. He made a very good impression in the FIL, depending on how spring training goes he could get a Clearwater assignment out of the gate next spring, which I think is very likely.

Twenty-year-old Greg Pickett is yet another sweet-swinging lefty power hitter in the system. He had a very nice year at Williamsport hitting .271/.343/.403 in 221 at bats and hit six homers while driving in 25. He's a big fella at 6'4", 215 lbs. and was the club's eighth round selection in the 2015 draft. Greg missed all of the 2016 season due to an illness but bounced back very well this year. He's a converted outfielder and has had his share of challenges defensively at first base both receiving and directly fielding the ball, something he's worked hard at improving. Greg has the offensive side of the game to advance along with an excellent work ethic, and I'd expect him to be the regular first baseman at Lakewood next summer while also getting at bats as a DH.

Luis Encarnacion is also just 20 years old and was once projected as a big-time power prospect. He's never really found a defensive position, which was even more delayed last fall when he suffered a broken ankle in Florida Instructional League play. Defensively he just doesn't move well and when he has gotten in the lineup it's been as a DH. Luis only got 75 at bats last summer and didn't put up good numbers in his second stint at Williamsport. He did hit very well in a brief four-game stint with the Clearwater Threshers when he filled in there back in July. He's only accumulated 605 at bats in his four-year minor league career, and at this point a continuation of employment should definitely be a concern. However, he may get another shot next summer to prove his way.

Twenty-three-year-old Quincy Nieporte, the club's 26th round selection this summer from Florida State, had an excellent first year in the GCL. He hit .299/.355/.494 in 154 at bats with 5 homers and 35 RBIs. I'd expect Quincy to at a minimum be assigned to Lakewood next summer with Clearwater also being a possibility.

Twenty-year-old Edwin Rodriquez has shown flashes of power in his four pro seasons but hasn't yet been afforded an opportunity to play regularly in his career other than in the DSL when he first signed. He's capable of also playing the outfield. He's a personable young man, I'm hopeful he gets a true chance next season.

Brian Mims, a 21-year-old, was the club's 21st round selection out of UNC Wilmington in the 2017 draft. He saw limited action for Williamsport getting just 121 at bats and playing mostly second base, however at season's end he was playing first base. He could be slated to return to the CrossCutters next summer as the primary first baseman.

Here's a look at Second Base:

The Big Club:

Cesar Hernandez, at 27, has established himself as a very solid major league player. He's produced a slash line of .294/.373/.421 with an OPS of .793 in 577 plate appearances in 2017. That's following a 2016 year when he hit .294/.371/.393/.764 in 622 plate appearances. Those are very good numbers. Hernandez has also shown excellent range at second base and has an above-average arm for the position - in fact, he has a shortstop-caliber arm. He is lightning fast but doesn't use his speed as an advantage to steal bases, a part of the struggles he still has with the base running aspect of the game. He will still do some head-scratching things on occasion, but the majority of his game is very good. Hernandez is a guy who should be a very productive player for at least another 7-8 years. His nine home runs reflect an increase in power and his 26 doubles are also a career high. If the organization didn't have a potential super star in the wings at Triple-A there would be no talk of trading such a productive player, but indeed they do and Hernandez may end up with a new organization in 2018.

The Minors:

Scott Kingery is just 23 years old. He was the Phillies second round draft pick in the 2015 draft out of the University of Arizona. Kingery earned the 2017 Paul Owens Award, which is given annually to the best minor league player in the Phillies system. Last season the award was shared by Rhys Hoskins and Dylan Cozens. In 132 games this summer he hit .304/.359/.530 with an OPS of .889 and bopped 26 home runs, drove in 65, had 29 doubles, eight triples and 29 stolen bases. He's an excellent defender at second base, has excellent range and a strong arm, and while he's not as strong as Hernandez, he's definitely above average. He turns the double play at second base better than anyone I've ever seen, with super-quick hands and feet. This kid can be a very special player for a very long time. He's got all the intangibles as well, a smart ball player and excellent base runner. I think he's every bit ready to be a major leaguer right now, and I also think he's an elite second baseman that could also play other positions if need be. But to me, it would be a waste of his overall skills to move him off second base. I see him as the Phillies second baseman for the next 10-to-12 years.

Jesmuel Valentin is also just 23 years old. He was the starter at Lehigh Valley until he suffered a season-ending injury to his left shoulder in mid-May. Valentin has produced solid stats during his six-year minor league career with a .261/.345/.382/.726 slash line in 1,593 at bats. Jesmuel isn't as strong defensively as Hernandez and Kingery but can certainly play the position well enough to be a solid contributor. He's got decent speed, but similar to Hernandez, doesn't use it as a base stealer with only 49 in his career in 443 games. Jesmuel had an outstanding spring training and almost made the big club out of camp as a utility man, he may become that in the future but for now I think it's prudent to keep him as a second baseman and see how he progresses.

Eliezar Alvarez was acquired in September from the St Louis Cardinals organization in the Juan Nicasio trade. He's 22-years-old and his career numbers very much align to Valentin's. Eliezar has hit .285/.360/.431/.791 in 1,158 minor league at bats. He had a breakout season in 2016 at the Single-A level for Peoria when he hit .323/.404/.476/.879 in 433 at bats with 36 doubles and 36 stolen bases. He got injured this May when he suffered a high ankle sprain and basically missed the remainder of the season. The notes I've read about him indicate he has excellent offensive tools in both bat and foot speed but isn't a strong fielder and doesn't have a strong enough arm to play anywhere but second base. The Cardinals skipped him over the High-A level and put him on the Double-A roster this season, where he struggled before being injured.

Twenty-four-year-old Drew Stankiewicz put up very solid numbers this summer between Reading and Lehigh Valley. He hit .280/.364/.421/.784 in 328 at bats playing 81 of his 107 games at second base. The 2014 11th round draft pick out of Arizona State is a gamer and heady player who by all accounts is well regarded by teammates. He's targeted for a return to Reading I would think and should challenge for a starting role there.

Clearwater ended the summer with 21-year-old Grenny Cumana and 22-year-old Jose Antequera splitting time at second base after Stankiewicz was promoted to Reading.

Neither young man excelled as Antequera hit just .170 in 88 at bats and Cumana .243 in 301 at bats.

Daniel Brito at 19 years old was the regular second baseman for Low-A level Lakewood. He played well early in the season but seemingly wore down as the summer progressed. Daniel hit .239/.298/.318/.615 in 447 at bats. He's a very good prospect who hits left handed and has a decent glove as well at second base. I believe he will repeat at Lakewood in 2018 similar to what Carlos Tocci and Deivi Grullon did at his age.

Twenty-two-year-old Jake Scheiner split time between second and third base for Williamsport this summer, playing 31 of the 55 games he participated in at second. He's the team's 2017 fourth round pick out of the University of Houston and is primarily known for offense, as he led Houston in home runs, RBIs and batting average on his way to being named an All-American in addition to earning a spot on the American Athletic Conference All-Academic team. He had a decent first pro season slashing .250/.317/.377/.694 in 236 at bats, made even more impressive by the fact he played through a hamstring injury for a good part of the year. He's a guy the Phillies see as being very versatile, similar to Ben Zobrist as far as his versaitilty. I believe he will begin 2018 at Clearwater, bypassing Lakewood, and will see the majority of his time there as a second baseman.

Twenty-year-old Jesus Azuaje was the team's 25th round selection in the 2017 draft out of Glendale Community College. He only got 78 at bats this year at Williamsport, playing 16 games as the second baseman. I'd expect he will return to the CrossCutters next summer.

Brayan Gonzalez as a 17-year-old was the regular at second base for the 2017 GCL Phillies. He didn't disappoint as he hit .269/.331/.388/.719 in 134 at bats with 10 doubles. He's a switch hitter and is acknowledged as having very good hands as a fielder. Given his age it wouldn't be a surprise if he repeated the GCL in 2018 however if he does well in 2018 spring training/XST he might earn a ticket to Williamsport.

Nineteen-year-old Jesus Henriquez is a very good hitter. That said, the task at hand is to find him a position he can play comfortably. This summer for the GCL Phillies he saw action at both second and third base, plus he has also played the outfield and first base previously. Jesus is a switch hitter, but I like him more from the left side where he has a very smooth line drive swing. I could see him in Williamsport next summer, it's just a question of at which position.

Seventeen-year-old Nicolas Torres had an outstanding season for the DSL Phillies White club. He hit .333/.383/.421/.804 in 240 at bats with 13 doubles, three triples and 11 stolen bases. Nicolas has very good speed and projects as a leadoff-type hitter, akin to Cesar Hernandez. I would think he plays stateside next summer in the GCL.

Depth of the Organization - Shortstop

The Big Club:

Although he didn't win the award, 27-year-old Freddy Galvis played Gold Glove-caliber shortstop this summer. The statistics may not bear it out but watching him play every day sure does. He makes ALL the plays, both the spectacular and the routine. He's as steady of a fielding influence at shortstop as anyone I've seen, and we've seen some good ones wear the Phillies jersey. Freddy is a free agent after the 2018 season, and that, along with concerns about his offense, may make him not as valued for a trade by others. His career slash line is .245/.287/.372 with a .659 OPS. In 2017 he hit .255/.309/.382 with a .690 OPS in 663 plate appearances. One other huge factor is leadership and likability, both of which he has going for him.

JP Crawford has played just 23 games in the big leagues. The 22-year-old slashed .214/.356/.300 with a .656 OPS in 87 plate appearances in the Show during 2017. He walked 16 times and struck out 22 times. He's got a very strong arm and even at 6'2" he's a graceful fielder at short, second and third base, as he was given chances at each spot this during his rookie debut. I don't think he's as gifted of a fielder as Galvis at the SS position, but on the other hand that's a pretty high standard. JP has been a career .270/.367/.391 hitter with a .759 OPS in 2,034 minor league at bats. He's also recorded 311 walks and 340 strikeouts. This season he had the worst slump of his career to start the year with Lehigh Valley but recovered nicely and earned his big league promotion. Even with the slump he led the International League in walks with 79 and posted a very good .351 OBP. The other thing that stands out about him is he's a consistent winner. Most every club he plays on wins more games than they lose, which I'd say is a good thing. His swing gets a bit long at times and he has a tendency to back-leg the approach but when he's short and quick through the ball he's the perfect definition of a number two hitter given his patience. I believe he's in the big leagues to stay but the role initially could be akin to what Javier Baez did for the Cubs in 2016, one where he plays multiple positions, and I think he's more than ok with doing that.

The Minors:

Angelo Mora took over at shortstop for Lehigh Valley after Crawford was promoted. The 24-year-old has played more of a utility role during his seven-year minor league career than as a position regular with action at second base, shortstop, third base and the outfield. He's been solid defensively at each spot and has posted a .258/.311/.365 line in 2,219 at bats with an OPS of .677. This summer he hit .291/.334/.435 with an OPS of 769 in 398 at bats. He was a minor league free agent this offseason and signed with the Baltimore Orioles for 2018.

Twenty-three-year-old Malquin Canelo was the regular shortstop for Reading this year and hit .226/.301/.339 with a .640 OPS in 389 at bats, but he also was a bit erratic in the field, committing 23 fielding errors. Malquin can make the spectacular play but needs to work on his consistency in order to progress as an everyday shortstop. He's shown flashes of being able to do so, but now it's repetition where the work is needed. With Crawford in the Show to begin 2018 and Mora moving on to another organization, there will be a void at the shortstop position for Lehigh Valley and it would seem Canelo will get a crack at it, although signing a minor league free agent or even having utility player Pedro Florimon man the position are also very real possibilities.

Twenty-four-year-old Emmanuel Marrero, the club's 2014 seventh round draft pick, began the year as Clearwater's every day shortstop and played 87 games there before ending the season with 16 games at third base. He made 13 errors at short, mostly throwing. He hit .252/.310/.359 with an OPS of .669 in 365 at bats, which are all higher numbers than his four-year career totals. I'd assume he will be given a shot at the Reading job next year if it's decided to move Canelo up a notch.

Twenty-year-old Jose Gomez was acquired by the Phillies in the Pat Neshek trade from the Rockies organization. He was tearing up the Low-A level South Atlantic League hitting .324/.374/.437 with a .811 OPS for the Rockies' Asheville affiliate. He finished the season at Clearwater, getting 92 at bats and hitting .250 playing exclusively shortstop in his 22 games there. Jose is a very good offensive player with a .312/.372/.400 slash line and an OPS of .771 in 1,146 minor league at bats. He's also played second and third base and could project as a "super utility" player, however I think the Phillies want to see him at shortstop. He's likely back in Clearwater next summer.

Nineteen-year-old Arquimedes Gamboa is a name to watch for in the organization. He's a slick fielder at shortstop possessing all the defensive tools to advance to the major leagues. He's got excellent hands, an above-average arm and baseball savvy. Offensively, he hit .261/.328/.378 with a .705 OPS in 307 at bats as he missed time during the summer due to injury, but he posted a .375 batting average in his last 10 games of the year. He also ended the year with a 14-game hitting streak where he went 23 for 55 (batting at a .418 clip). Given his age it would not be a surprise to see him repeat next year at Lakewood or at least start 2018 there as it was just his first year of full season play. With a good winter ball season and decent showing in spring training, he could push his way to Clearwater as well.

Twenty-year-old Nick Maton, the club's seventh round draft pick this summer, saw the brunt of the action for Williamsport at shortstop playing 57 games there. He hit .252/.350/.333 with a .683 OPS in 210 at bats. Nick committed nine errors in 264 chances. He should get a shot at least at the Lakewood roster in spring training.

The GCL Phillies roster had three shortstops who each saw playing time:

Eighteen-year-old Jonathan Guzman is almost a clone of Gamboa. Guzman hit .248/.299/.320 with an OPS of .619 in 153 at bats. He wore down as the season progressed as he spent the entire XST/GCL seasons in the heat at Clearwater but also played six games at Williamsport to begin their year. This was only his second year as a pro, and one would expect he's at Williamsport next summer full-time.

Twenty-one-year-old Dalton Guthrie played in only nine games after signing this summer. He was the team's sixth round draft pick out of the University of Florida. I'd expect he might leapfrog Low-A ball out of spring training and open 2018 as the regular shortstop for Clearwater. He's a superior defender.

Nineteen-year-old Jake Holmes was the team's 11th round pick this summer and was signed to an over-slot bonus. He's a big kid at 6'3", 185 lbs., and showed good pop this summer in 107 at bats. He slashed .252/.331/.355 with an OPS of

.686. He played exclusively at third base during FIL and that's likely where he's going to be playing in 2018.

Edgar Made, Jose Tortolero and Christian Valerio are 17-year-olds who played in the DSL this year. They could come stateside to the GCL next year.

The Phillies also signed 16-year-old Dominican shortstop Luis Garcia this summer to a $2.5 million bonus. He was rated by Baseball America as the 12th-best international prospect in this year's pool. He participated in the 2017 Florida Instructional League and there's little doubt he's headed for a GCL Phillies roster next summer.

Depth of the Organization - Third Base

The Big Club:

Twenty-five-year-old Maikel Franco is being seen by many in a different light than the 23-year-old version who made his rookie debut in 2015. He was considered a long-term fixture then as the team's third baseman and one with a very bright future. So what's changed? A lower-than-expected output in 2016 has been followed up by an even more disappointing 2017. Maikel hit just .230/.281/.409 with a .690 OPS in 623 plate appearances with 24 home runs and 76 RBIs. The sabermetrics folks will point out that he hit the ball harder and had a case of the "at 'em balls" in his at bats, and they will also highlight that he has struck out less (17 percent this year compared to 18 percent in 2016). Franco, by all accounts, is an upbeat person who's well liked and is a very diligent worker, so it's not for lack of effort that his numbers are down. The decision at hand is whether the 2017 version is the player he's destined to be, or if indeed the stardom that folks projected for him very early on (dating back to June of 2010 when he first signed as a raw 17-year-old) still projects. Maikel's boyhood idol was Adrian Beltre, and when comparing Beltre's age 24/25 season he hit .240/.290/.424 in 559 at bats, but followed that with his best season as a major leaguer, hitting 48 home runs and driving in 121 runs while hitting .334. Franco certainly has the physical tools to succeed, it's a matter of whether he can make the adjustments in his approach that is the debate. 2017 Hitting Coach Matt Stairs believes he can, but I'm not so sure all are on that same page. Trading Maikel this offseason may not be the most prudent move as it would be a situation of selling low given his down season; however if a decent trade offer is made by another club I'm sure the Phillies will listen.

The Minors:

The Lehigh Valley Triple-A club didn't have a regular third baseman so to speak this year, the closest person to that description was 29-year-old Hector Gomez, and he spent multiple stints on the DL amassing only 212 at bats and hitting just .236/.260/.425. Hector is likely headed elsewhere in 2018.

Twenty-five-year-old Mitch Walding is destined to be the Lehigh Valley third baseman in 2018. He hit 25 home runs at the Double-A level for Reading but his slash line of .236/.327/.516 in 351 at bats and 127 strikeouts weren't encouraging numbers. Mitch was injured late in the season when he broke his nose in a collision with catcher Chace Numata. The 2011 fifth round pick has always been an excellent defender at third but his hitting isn't major league ready. His career numbers of .240/.330/.375 in 2,208 at bats indicate that the slash line at Reading in 2017 might just about be where he will be. The 25 homers represent half of his 51 career taters in his six-year pro career. He's a good young man so I'm pulling for him to have a breakout year all around in 2018.

Twenty-six-year-old Damek Tomscha had a very good summer playing at both Clearwater and Reading. He hit .307/.386/.439 with an .825 OPS in 374 at bats (201 at Clearwater, 159 at Reading). He also tallied 11 homers and 52 RBIs and his strikeout rate of 15 percent was consistent with his career average. This is the first offseason that he's eligible for the Rule 5 Draft and it's not out of the question that another club may take a shot at him. He's primarily a third baseman but also can play first base and left field. I'd expect that he gets a chance in spring training to earn a spot on the Lehigh Valley roster with Reading as the fallback plan. He's a very good hitter with a .282/.370/.417 career line in 1,356 at bats.

Twenty-three-year-old Zach Green missed basically the entire year while recovering from Tommy John surgery. The third round pick from the 2012 draft played in the Arizona Fall League to make up for the missed action. He did accumulate 198 at bats between GCL/Clearwater/Reading in 2017 and hasn't ever had a season with more than 354 at bats, due to injuries throughout his six-year career. If he can stay healthy he's still got a chance to advance as he's got an excellent swing and can hit the ball consistently hard. I think the organization sees more value in him as a third baseman although he has also played first base. I'd expect he starts the 2018 season with Reading as their starter at third base.

Twenty-two-year-old Jan Hernandez (2013 third round pick) started the 2017 season as the regular third baseman for Clearwater. He struggled defensively and was moved to the outfield later in the year. Hernandez committed 17 errors in 103 chances at third base, coming off a 2016 season where he had 18 errors in 207 chances. It's been a consistent issue for him as he made 79 errors in 479 career chances as a third baseman. Jan did show power potential again this summer as he slugged 16 home runs, following a 10-homer effort in 2016 at Lakewood. His slash line was not good though as he hit just .212/.287/.415 in 316 at bats. My guess is he repeats Clearwater and more than likely as an outfielder if he returns there. He performed well in the outfield, showing an accurate throwing arm.

Twenty-one-year-old Luke Williams (a 2015 third round draft pick) struggled offensively this summer in his first full season assignment at Lakewood. He posted a .216/.269/.264 slash line in 402 at bats with an OPS of .533. He did steal 29 bases in 31 attempts which tied him for second-most among all Phillies minor leaguers. He played outfield in the Colombian Winter League this fall as well as seeing time there and at second base during Florida Instructs.

Depth of the Organization – Catcher

The Big Club:

Cameron Rupp completed his third season in the Show this year. The 29-year-old played in 88 games this summer, 17 less than the year before, and posted a slash line of .217/.299/.417 with an OPS of .716 in 295 at bats. He hit 14 home runs, two less than in 2016 when he got 389 at bats. Cameron matched his strikeout total of 114 of 2016 in 94 fewer at bats. He's regarded as a very good teammate and certainly showed improvement defensively this year, specifically in his blocking skills. While it seems he wouldn't be considered as an everyday player at this point, one question to ask is whether his defensive skills are solid enough as a backup. From my perspective, I think he's certainly qualified for that role and given the lack of truly skilled receivers in the game today he's also someone who could grab a more prominent playing status. The decision point as to what role he assumes may just come down to a Phillies spring training competition. He could also be packaged in a deal this offseason to a club looking for catching help.

Jorge Alfaro was very successful offensively this summer after his call up on August 4. He posted a .318/.360/.514 line with an .874 OPS in 29 games and 107 at bats with five home runs and 14 RBIs. The 24-year-old struck out 33 times, adding to a significant improvement from his 84 games at Lehigh Valley where he hit just .241/.291/.358 with a .649 OPS in 324 at bats. However, the focus at Lehigh Valley this summer was on defensive improvement. Jorge showed he's certainly not a finished product in receiving the ball and shifting his feet on defensive blocking of balls in the dirt, but he certainly has the skills to get there and is a renowned hard worker. At this point he will be a major league defensive work in progress as he's out of minor league options. The upside potential in his overall game is very high so he definitely will be on the 25-man roster next year and is likely the starter. The plan may include having a more defensive-minded mentor as a backup, or else carry a third catcher with the same type of characteristics.

Twenty-five-year-old Andrew Knapp may just be the best all-around catcher on the club at this point. He had a decent rookie year, hitting .257/.368/.368 with a .736 OPS in 171 at bats with three homers and 13 RBIs. The switch hitter had taken over the brunt of the catching duties before going on the DL on August 7 with a bruised right hand. He's better than serving as just a backup, so I could envision a co-catching role with Alfaro in 2018 with a third catcher also being on the club to allow Knapp and/or Alfaro to play an occasional game at first base. The other option is to send him to Lehigh Valley as the regular catcher there, as he has minor league options left, but that seems like a waste of talent. He could be dangled as available in a trade as well, where he is young enough to merit a decent return especially if coupled with others in a package deal.

The Minors:

Logan Moore was the Phillies' ninth round pick in the 2011 draft, and the 27-year-old has always been a stellar defender, perhaps the best in the entire system. This season he saw an increase in his playing time after Jorge Alfaro was promoted to the big leagues in early August, turning Moore into the primary catcher at Lehigh Valley. He hit .233/.310/.362 with a .672 OPS in 210 at bats with six homers and 31 RBIs. He's a career .223/.295/.324 hitter with an OPS of .618 in 1,499 at bats playing in 466 games over his seven-year career. He earned the right to become a minor league free agent but re-signed with the Phillies for 2018. I've always believed he is a major league-caliber catcher.

Nick Rickles is also 27 years old and also in his seventh season as a pro, as he was drafted by the Oakland A's in the 14th round of the 2011 draft. Nick was acquired by the Phillies this season from the Washington Nationals and played 26 games at Reading before finishing up with nine games at Lehigh Valley. Overall this summer he hit .258/.292/.422 with a .714 OPS in 37 games (128 at bats). He's a very good defensive catcher.

Chace Numata was the 14th round draft choice of the Phillies in the 2010 draft as a high school player from Pearl City, Hawaii. He earned free agent status last offseason and chose to re-sign with the Phillies on a one-year contract. Chace was the starting catcher at Reading before he suffered a concussion on July 26 in a collision with third baseman Mitch Walding. He didn't return to the active roster till August 8, where he hit .249/.318/.351 with an OPS of .668 in 84 games (305 at bats). Those are similar to his career numbers, and he's a good defensive receiver with perhaps the quickest release on throws as any catcher in the system. Chace signed with the Yankees in November as a minor league free agent.

Twenty-one-year-old Deivi Grullon completed his fifth year of pro ball this summer making him eligible for the Rule 5 draft. Deivi began the year at Clearwater as the regular catcher and was promoted to Reading on July 27 when Numata went on the DL, and he finished the season with the Fightin's. Overall Grullon hit .249/.283/.398 with an OPS of .681 in 94 games (354 at bats). He's got a very good arm and is well regarded as a signal caller and receiver. Once thought of as a top prospect, Grullon will likely be catching again at Reading next summer.

Edgar Cabral started the summer at Lakewood and was promoted to Clearwater on July 27 as a trickle-down effect of the Numata injury at Reading. The 22-year-old completed his third pro season after being the 11th round selection of the 2015 draft. He hit .260/.332/.357 with an .690 OPS in 91 games and 319 at bats. Cabral had a remarkable caught stealing rate, throwing out 44 of 91 would be base stealers, a .485 percentage! I'd expect him to open the 2018 season at Clearwater.

Austin Bossart also completed his third pro season this summer and spent time at both Clearwater and Reading. The 24-year-old 14th round pick from 2015 hit .245/.284/.332 with an OPS of .616 in 184 at bats in 55 games, all but one at Clearwater. He's also noted as a strong defender, and should compete for a job at Reading at the least this coming spring training with perhaps a backup role at Lehigh Valley also possible.

Twenty-two-year-old Henri Lartigue was the seventh round selection of the Phillies in the 2016 draft out of Ole Miss. He spent the 2017 season at Lakewood and hit .248/.292/.410 with an OPS of 702 in 94 games and 339 at bats with 23 doubles, four triples, eight home runs and knocking in 44 runs. I saw him in FIL play and was impressed with his take charge attitude behind the dish. Henri certainly will get a shot at the Clearwater roster this coming spring.

Twenty-two-year-old Colby Fitch was the team's 13th round draft pick this summer out of Louisville. He hit .266/.400/.413 with an OPS of .813 in 34 games (109 at bats) between Williamsport and Lakewood. Like Lartigue he's noted for his leadership abilities, and he likely plays again for the BlueClaws to start 2018.

Twenty-one-year-old Gregori Rivero got into 30 games for Lakewood this summer after playing eight at Williamsport. He hit .270/.292/.416 with an OPS of .708 in 137 at bats. He should compete once again for a role with the BlueClaws next spring.

Nineteen-year-old Rodolfo Duran completed his third pro season this summer, where he played 48 games and had 159 at bats for Williamsport, hitting .252/.298/.346 with a .644 OPS. He had nine errors and 13 passed balls this season and is back in the Florida Instructional League for a third fall. He might repeat Williamsport next summer but with a good spring training could earn a spot with Lakewood.

Twenty-one-year-old Nerluis Martinez struggled offensively this summer between Lakewood and Williamsport, hitting just .153/.187/.208 with an OPS of .395 in 72 at bats across 24 games. It would seem he's got to battle to maintain a roster spot in the organization this coming spring.

Three catchers split time for the GCL Phillies. 18-year-old Rafael Marchan played in 30 games and got 84 at bats hitting .238/.290/.298. 19-year-old Lenin Rodriquez played 32 games and got 61 at bats hitting .262/.408/.344, and 21-year-old Kipp Moore played in 32 games hitting .250/.344/.339 in 56 at bats. Marchan and Moore are participating in Florida Instructs this year. All three should compete for roles at Williamsport next spring.

Eighteen-year-old Carlos Oropeza had a very good season in the DSL hitting .271/.337/.358 with an OPS of .695 in 64 games, accumulating 218 at bats. His season earned him a spot in the Florida Instructional League. He's bigger than both Marchan and Rodriquez at 6'0", 170 lbs. and could bump ahead of them next spring for a role with the GCL Phillies.

There's a strong possibility the Phillies have two GCL teams next summer so 18-year-old Juan Mendez, who had a stellar offensive year for the DSL White club hitting .379/.411/.571 with an OPS of .982 in 39 games (140 at bats) with three homers and 26 RBIs, certainly has a real chance of coming stateside next year.

The Phillies signed Cesar Rodriquez and Oscar Gonzalez this summer from Venezuela. Rodriquez was the 42nd-ranked international prospect by Baseball America. They should compete with fellow teenagers Juan Aparicio, Ronald Torrealba and Freddy Barreto for spots in the GCL and DSL next summer.

Depth of the Organization - Outfielders

What was once a glaring weakness of the organization not so long ago, especially at the major league level, is now a very positive strength. The team ended the 2017 season with three young outfielders positioned as starters going into 2018 and roster flexibility to use other players in the outfield if needed. Here's a look at the outfield depth.

The Big Club:

Aaron Altherr, Odubel Herrera and Nick Williams not only give the Phillies a good offensive outlook, but also possess the defensive skills that will allow them to move around if needed. The 26-year-old Altherr hit .272/.340/.516 with an OPS of .856 in 372 at bats with 19 homers and 65 RBIs. Odubel hit .281/.325/.452 with a .778 OPS with 42 doubles, 14 homers and 56 RBIs in 526 at bats and Williams hit .288/.338/.473 with an OPS of .811 and 12 homers with 55 RBIs in 313 at bats. Those are some very good numbers, made even more impressive when it's noted that Odubel is just 25 and Nick is 24. These three could be big leaguers for at least another 10 years. One or more of them could be moved in an offseason trade, but if the Phillies opened 2018 with this trio as the starting group there's definite reason to be optimistic about how they will fare.

Veterans Daniel Nava, Hyun Soo Kim and Ty Kelly were the backups at season's end, along with Cameron Perkins. Nava and Kim are set to be free agents and Kelly declined assignment to Lehigh Valley after the season, becoming a free agent. Perkins hit just .182 in 88 big league at bats, but given the chance, I think the 27-year-old could stick as a fourth or fifth outfielder.

Rhys Hoskins showed that he can maneuver well enough out in left field if need be and that will certainly give new skipper Gabe Kapler added flexibility in writing out a lineup.

The Minors:

There is no one in the entire organization who has more power than 23-year-old Dylan Cozens. The young man struggled on offense for the first time in his six-year pro career this summer, hitting just .210/.301/.418 with an OPS of .719 in 476 at bats for Lehigh Valley. He did hit 27 homers and drove in 75 but struck out 194 times and saw his production in doubles drop from 38 the year before at Reading to just 12. The times I saw him he was over aggressive at the plate and more often than not "got himself out" as they say. Pitchers used his aggression against him especially on high pitches out of the zone that he continually chased. He's got real talent though, and I expect that he uses 2017 as a learning tool and busts out in 2018 with a more disciplined approach. He's strong enough to hit 25 homers by accident, which is basically what happened this summer, but he's capable of hitting 35 to 40 with as many doubles. I'm pulling for him to do just that as he can be a special player who, if he gets it right mentally, can dominate physically. Look for him to repeat AAA again to at least start in 2018.

Roman Quinn was off to a decent start at Lehigh Valley before having his season end to yet another injury. He hit .274/.344/.389 in 175 at bats. The 24-year-old was sent home early from 2017 Dominican Winter League play as he struggled there. He will be back in big league camp next spring and has a shot at sticking with the club as a fourth outfielder.

Andrew Pullin, Carlos Tocci and Herlis Rodriquez all struggled at the AAA level in limited at bats. The 24-year-old Pullin hit just .231 at Lehigh Valley in 238 at bats after posting a .308

average at Reading in 266 at bats with 22 doubles. He also hit another 21 doubles for the IronPigs, ending the season with 43. He's a line drive/gaps hitter, and should return to Lehigh Valley next season if not taken in the Rule 5 draft, as he wasn't put on the initial 2018 40-man roster. If he returns I see no reason to expect that he won't put up good numbers. I think he's a Greg Gross/Del Unser-type lefty hitter who will be a good major league bat off the bench as his career progresses. Tocci hit just .189 in 53 ABs for Lehigh Valley after posting stellar numbers at Reading. He's just 22, is an excellent defender in center field and has all the tools. He too should return to Lehigh Valley to begin 2018, assuming he's not taken in the Rule 5 draft as he was also left unprotected. Herlis Rodriquez finished his seventh pro season this past summer and is eligible to become a minor league free agent. He may look to another organization for a better opportunity.

Cord Sandberg, Zachary Coppola and Jiandido Tromp ended the year as the primary outfield group for AA level Reading. However, Sandberg suffered a late season injury that forced manager Greg Legg to play one of his infielders out on the grass to complete the schedule. Sandberg is just 22, he strained his UCL which didn't require surgery and was at Clearwater during FIL play rehabbing, where he said he's on track to start 2018 healthy. Cord had a solid summer hitting .268/.309/.431 in 362 at bats at three levels. He's Rule 5 eligible this year but should be back at Reading for next season and will very likely compete for a starting job. He has good overall skills, but just needs to pull them together to get back on the prospect radar.

Tromp had a very good season hitting .284/.328/.482 with an OPS of .810 in 465 at bats with 18 homers and 64 RBIs, and also had 32 doubles. The 24-year-old should be in the mix at Lehigh Valley next season. Coppola is just 23 years old and began the summer with Clearwater before finishing up at Reading, hitting a combined .285/.357/.328 with a .685 OPS in 485 at bats (325 of those were at Reading). The slugging percentage is telling as he's a pure singles hitter, as he had only 17 extra base hits. I think he's back at Reading to at least start the 2018 season.

Cornelius Randolph, Jan Hernandez and Mark Laird ended the season as the outfield crew at High-A Clearwater. Randolph also played in the Arizona Fall League. The 20-year-old left handed hitter was tasked with focusing on pulling the ball to his power side in 2017 and was instructed not to worry about stats or strikeouts. He did very well, hitting a career-high 13 home runs and driving in 55 RBIs with a line of .250/.338/.402 in 440 at bats while drawing 55 walks. Randolph is slated for the left field job in Reading next year, and I think he's going to have a breakout season. The young man is a pure hitter.

Hernandez moved to the outfield from third base after struggling defensively at the hot corner, and he fared very well as a right fielder, displaying a plus arm while picking up five assists. The 22-year-old hit 16 home runs but also hit just .212 in 316 at bats, so I'd expect he's back at Clearwater for 2018.

Mark Laird is a very similar player to Zach Coppola, the 24-year-old hit .286/.338/.365 with a .702 OPS in 406 at bats but had just 23 extra base hits. He's a very good outfielder, certainly deserves an opportunity to be in the mix at Reading in 2018.

Twenty-two-year-old Jose Pujols had a very bad season hitting just .194 in 325 at bats and striking out 150 times. He needs a big spring to return again to Clearwater.

Lakewood's end-of-year outfield was Adam Haseley, Mickey Moniak and Jesus Alastre with Austin Listi seeing some action in left field when not at first base. The 20-year-old Alastre put up really good numbers at .301/.351/.391 with a .742 OPS in 156 at bats. He had similar numbers at Williamsport in 2016 - not a lot of pop but an on-base machine.

Moniak ended his first full pro season at .236/.284/.341 with a .625 OPS in 466 at bats, as the 19-year-old simply wore down over the long summer. He showed all the skills that got him drafted number one overall in the 2016 draft but was just inconsistent. It's very probable he starts 2018 again in Lakewood. With a lot of time ahead of him in his development, there's no need to panic.

Haseley also wore down as the summer went on. He played at three levels and hit .284/.357/.405 in 215 at bats with a .761 OPS and 18 extra base hits. Adam was also in Florida Instructs and played both left and center field there. He's ticketed for Clearwater to start 2018.

Yahir Gurrola, Josh Stephen and Jhailyn Ortiz seem to be the most likely guys to move up next spring to Lakewood from Williamsport. Gurrola had a very productive Instructional League campaign after hitting .287/.354/.366 in 202 at bats between GCL and the Williamsport, and he's got really good speed as well. Stephen also had a good Fall Instructs camp after getting 239 at bats for Williamsport. I think he's in line to have a big summer next year. Ortiz could be the most exciting prospect in the entire system. The 18-year-old hit .302/.401/.560 with a .961 OPS in 159 at bats with eight homers and 30 RBIs. He combines power with hitting skills and will work pitchers for walks as well. It should be a fun summer in Lakewood in 2018 for Ortiz - he's for real.

Malvin Matos shouldn't be lost in the shuffle, as the 21-year-old is a solid player who got a lot of innings as the center fielder in Williamsport after Haseley went to Lakewood. Next spring will be a key one for him to earn an advancement.

Nineteen-year-old Ben Pelletier had a big season in the GCL and should at least earn a spot with Williamsport in 2018 with Lakewood also being a possibility. Simon Muzziotti and Keudy Boccio are both 18-year-olds who could repeat GCL but also have the skills to move up to Williamsport next summer. Kevin Markham and Danny Mayer could both jump up as high as Clearwater out of spring training.

Julio Francisco and Carlos De La Cruz were both DSL players in Florida Fall Instructs and likely will play 2018 in the GCL. I like Francisco's bat, as he is a good looking hitter.

Depth of the Organization - Starting Pitching

The Phillies supposedly don't have an "Ace" or number one starter amongst their more immediate big league-ready ranks of starters, but who's to say that fella won't emerge from the very good quality of depth in the system. I doubt many folks in Houston believed Dallas Kuechel was an "Ace" when he finished his last full minor league season in 2011 with a 4.12 ERA, including posting a 7.50 ERA in seven starts at Triple-A that year, but yet just four seasons later he was a 20-game winner in the Show. And this is a guy whose fastball sits upper 90' at best. Here's a look at our starting pitching depth.

The Big Leagues:

Aaron Nola had a breakout season in 2017 posting a 3.54 ERA in 168 IP in 27 starts. He pitched with confidence, poise and command after spending some time with rehab pitching coach Ray Burris down in Clearwater in late April. Burris told Nola to trust his fastball and to incorporate his legs more into his delivery. It's the mechanics of hip rotation that the development system emphasizes with the minor leaguers. When Nola came off the DL in mid-May he was a different pitcher, with increased velocity and a higher tendency to utilize his fastball to set up his devastating curve ball, which became an even more effective pitch. The 24-year-old pitched like an "Ace" from that point on and the results followed. He's a cool kid, always friendly to chat with and very patient with fan requests, and his outward demeanor on the mound is similar but he's a battler out there as well. I think he can be the "Ace" we seemingly lack, and I think 2018 could be a very big year for this young man.

So... one spot on the big league club is stabilized but the remaining 4 spots are wide open. Here are the guys who will battle for those spots in spring training:

Jerad Eickhoff: I don't think the 27-year-old was ever healthy this season, including in spring training. Jerad threw 197 innings in 2016 but scuffled through 128 in 2017 and his ERA went to 4.71 from 3.65. I still think he's a quality starter and very capable of bouncing back in 2018. I can see him earning a rotation spot in spring training if he's healthy.

Vince Velasquez: the 25-year-old also suffered a season-ending injury in 2018 with numbness in his hand. He only threw 72 innings in 15 starts and had a high 5.13 ERA. From my perspective I think he's better suited for a bullpen role with the big fastball he possesses. He reminds me of Ryan Madsen, who just didn't have the makeup as a starter but excelled in shorter stints when he could just fire away. Velasquez to me could be another Archie Bradley whom the Diamondbacks moved out of the rotation into the pen and he excelled. The Phillies seem insistent on making Vince a starter though, and to me that's not the right path.

Nick Pivetta: the 24-year-old ended up making 26 big league starts this summer. In some he was very good, in others he was bad. Nick has a big-time arm with a fastball that can sit mid 90s and reach the upper levels, and his secondary pitches can be also very good but he struggles commanding them and repeating his delivery. He struck out 140 batters in 133 IP but had a 6.01 ERA. Unlike Velasquez I think he's got the mix to be a quality starting pitcher, and hopefully taking his lumps in 2017 makes him stronger and more effective next season. This is a guy who's only had 10 starts at the AAA level, so it might be determined in spring training that he should go back there for more experience, especially if he doesn't show more command in spring training camp. However, my guess is he will be part of the 2018 big league rotation. The young man has big-time upside if he can figure out the mechanical and emotional parts of the job.

Ben Lively: the 25-year-old made 15 big league starts and posted a 4-7 record with a 4.26 ERA in 88 IP. He's a fighter on the bump who so far in his career usually wins more often than not. Ben doesn't have electric stuff but certainly has enough to pitch in the Show. He seems to be a guy who's destined to always be battling for a spot in the rotation but also some who could be sent to AAA. Lively has done all he can do at the minor league level, as he's a Paul Owens Award winner already. I like his moxy, demeanor and approach of "you gotta hit my pitch to beat me." He will fight for a job in r2018 spring training somewhere if not here.

Jake Thompson: the 23-year-old put up decent numbers in his 11 big league games this summer posting a 3-2 record with a 3.88 ERA in 46 IP. He walked too many batters (22) and sometimes got out of sync when things went awry, but generally he did a nice job when given the chance this year. He actually struggled more at the AAA level this year than in the big leagues. It was an up-and-down season for Jake for sure, he suffered a hand injury early on in spring pre-camp workouts and never seemed to recover fully from that setback. From my perspective he's a sinker ball pitcher who gets in trouble when he tries to pitch like a four-seam fastball. He can reach mid 90s with the four-seam fastball but it comes out of his hand flat, whereas the sinker, when he's focused with it, has good run and downward slope. Although, he has not really shown that good sinker in the bigs yet. To me that's the key as to whether he can be a successful big league pitcher: focusing on becoming a heavy sinker baller is the key to his success, he's just got to convince himself of that.

The Minors:

2017 was a lost season for 23-year-old Zach Eflin. He had offseason surgery on both knees and then developed shoulder stiffness later in the summer which ended his year. He posted a 1-5 record with a 6.16 ERA in 64 Major League innings after posting 55 innings in the minors. He's got really good stuff when he's healthy so I'm hoping that 2017 was just a season of recovery and that he comes back strong this spring. Of all the upper level guys other than Nola I believe Zach has the best repertoire and could be a very effective big league starter. Given he's just 23 there's plenty of time for that to develop.

Drew Anderson is another 23-year-old with big potential. The right-hander pitched in two major league games this summer and should be slated for a starting spot at Lehigh Valley in 2018 after going 9-4 with a 3.59 ERA in 107 innings pitched at Double-A Reading. He's got a mid-90s fastball and an above average curve, but the third pitch is his work in progress. It's presently a changeup or hard slider. If Anderson continues to progress as he has the past two seasons he's a guy who could see real big league time in 2018 and could stick as part of the rotation when given the chance.

Elniery Garcia was out of sight, out of mind after incurring an 80-game suspension for violating the major league PED policy. His season consisted of just seven games after the suspension was served, and he posted a 2-1 record with a 1.75 ERA in 30 innings. The 22-year-old lefty pitched in the Arizona Fall League to make up for the lost time. When he's on he can reach mid 90s with the fastball and has decent secondary pitches with movement. He's no longer on the 40-

man roster. Elniery should at the least be part of the Reading rotation next year, as he's got a big league arm and if he can use the suspension as a learning tool, he is someone who could also become a big league starter in the not-so-distant future.

Twenty-three-year-old Tom Eshelman won the Paul Owens Award as the best Phillies Minor League Pitcher in 2017. He was outstanding going 13-3 with a 2.40 ERA in 150 IP with just 18 walks. It wouldn't figure he would begin 2018 as part of the big league staff, but hey the Yankees didn't think Jordan Montgomery would make their club this year but he had a great spring and a very solid season for them. Eshelman is a true pitcher, his fastball sits 90-92 and he has three off-speed pitches, all of which he can throw for strikes at any time. He is a smart pitcher who uses his strengths against his opponents' weaknesses and is also a battler. He reminds me of the Cubs' Kyle Hendricks in the way he pitches and approaches hitters. He should get a big league camp invite this spring. It's only his fourth pro season coming up so there's no need to put him on the 40-man roster yet, but that doesn't mean he won't pitch himself onto it though.

Brandon Leibrandt had a very good comeback season in 2017 after an injury-plagued year before. The Florida State product went 11-5 with a 3.62 ERA in 25 starts (136 IP) between Reading and Lehigh Valley. He could become the lefty version of Eshelman with a bit less command. He's also a low 90s fastball pitcher with two secondary offerings who pitches to contact. Brandon is Rule 5 eligible this offseason, and some team may give the 24-year-old a look if he's left unprotected.

Twenty-three-year-old Jose Taveras earned a spot on the 40-man roster for 2018. He went 9-6 at three levels with a 2.22 ERA in 154 IP, including a 3-1 record with a 1.32 ERA in seven starts for Lehigh Valley (41 IP). He uses a full repertoire of pitches to get batters out, including mixing deliveries and changing speeds. He's fun to watch pitch as he shows emotion on the bump, and he might just be a big leaguer in 2018.

Franklyn Kilome also was awarded a spot on the 2018 40-man roster. The 22-year-old has big time projection. He went 7-7 with a 2.83 ERA in 24 starts (127 IP) between Clearwater and Reading this summer, striking out 103 batters which is indicative of the approach he took this year of getting batters out in other ways besides a strikeout. He's got a really big arm, 95-98 range fastball and a nasty slider and changeup. One thing I noticed when I saw him this year was his pitches seemed flatter than last year – I don't know if that was a result of mechanics but it did seem to lessen the life on the heater. He should be part of the Reading rotation to start 2018.

Jacob Waguespack put himself on the prospect radar with a breakout 2017 season. The 23-year-old undrafted free agent began the season in Clearwater's bullpen but was moved to the starting rotation and ended the summer with a 9-7 record and a 3.42 ERA in 105 IP with 108 strikeouts between Clearwater and Reading. He ended the year making a very impressive start in the playoffs for Triple-A Lehigh Valley in a game where he threw seven innings allowing only one run on three hits while striking out seven batters. The big right-hander saw his velocity jump to 92-94 and used two solid off-speed pitches to round out his mix. He was a starter in winter ball in the 2016 Colombian Winter league and I truly believe that helped him during this past summer. Jacob should at a minimum start the year at Reading with a very good chance of advancing to Lehigh Valley either during the season or directly out of spring training.

Twenty-three-year-old Cole Irvin pitched at two levels in 2017, going 9-9 with a 3.39 ERA in 151 innings pitched between Clearwater and Reading. He's a very smart pitcher, and my description of him is he's Jamie Moyer with a better fastball. Irvin sits 90-93 with the fastball but also has three off-speed pitches, including a one seam fastball grip that performs like a splitter. Cole likely begins 2017 in the Reading rotation again but is another young pitcher who could rise to the AAA level before season's end and even perhaps make an appearance in the big leagues.

Tyler Viza is still just 22 years old, and he has pitched "Up a Level" for most of his five-year pro career in regards to his age. He was a starter for full season Lakewood at just 19. This summer was his second at Reading and he posted 10 wins just as he did in 2016. Tyler struggled more this summer however with an ERA of 5.22 in 139 IP (2016 was 3.95 in 143 IP). I would think he's slotted for a shot at Lehigh Valley's rotation this spring. Perhaps a conversion to a Mark Leiter, Jr.-type role may be his destiny.

Clearwater ended the season with five outstanding prospects in their starting rotation. 21-year-old McKenzie Mills pitched only one game for the Threshers before the Phillies shut him down for the season, but the young lefty acquired from Washington in the Howie Kendrick trade went 12-2 with a 3.22 ERA in 120 IP for Hagerstown in the South Atlantic

League with 118 K's and just 18 walks before coming over to the Phillies. He was in Florida Instructs but didn't throw in any games there either. I did get a chance to chat with him and he's very excited about 2018. It's his Rule 5 season and he hopes to make a push for the upper levels. He likely begins at Clearwater but with success could move quickly to Reading.

Sixto Sanchez is the crown jewel of the system's pitching depth. The 19-year-old has a golden arm with ability to consistently reach 100 mph with the heater and also possesses mound presence and potential upper tier off-speed pitches. He too should begin the season at Clearwater but if he excels like he's expected to a mid-summer move up to Double-A could also be in the offering.

Twenty-two-year-old Seranthony Dominguez was as good as anyone in the system at the beginning of 2017, however injury setbacks limited his innings to just 67. He struck out 82 batters and posted a 3.72 ERA but after the injuries battled command issues and ended up with 34 walks. He was added to the 2018 40-man roster as arms that pop upper 90s and 100 on the heater are premium talents, and that's what he's capable of.

Jo Jo Romero had an outstanding 2017 season going 10-3 with a 2.17 ERA in 129 IP between Lakewood and Clearwater. He struck out 128 hitters while walking just 36 in his 23 starts. The 21-year-old lefty has a four-pitch repertoire including a fastball that sits at 92-94 MPH. He's a fast track guy and very likely gets a shot at the Reading rotation to begin 2018 with an eye on advancement during the season.

This young man is a very good pitcher who has major league skills already, and just needs some refinement.

Ranger Suarez is a 22-year-old lefty who also had a very strong 2017 campaign. He went 8-6 with a 2.27 ERA in 122 IP with 128 K's and just 35 walks between Lakewood and Clearwater. He wasn't as good at High-A as he was at Lakewood where he posted a 1.59 ERA in 85 IP. He was hit a bit more as a Thresher with a 3.82 ERA in 37 IP there, and I think he tired as the season went on. Suarez was pumping his fastball in the 95-96 range early in the year, and that fell a bit as the summer progressed. He's a true pitcher also as he has a very good slider and straight changeup as well. He is Rule 5 eligible this offseason and is another one who likely is put on the 40-man roster. He should also get a shot at the Reading rotation in spring training.

All 20-year-old Nick Fanti did in 2017 was throw two no hitters... actually if that's all he did it certainly would be impressive, but the lefty did much more. He went 9-2 with a 2.54 ERA in 120 IP with 121 K's and just 28 walks in a breakout first full season year as a pro. Of course, we might have expected his success as he was 7-0 with a 1.54 ERA the year before in the GCL. Nick doesn't overpower his opponents but has great movement on his pitches and hides the ball very well in his delivery. His off-speed pitches are superior in location and movement. He's certainly earned a shot at High-A Clearwater to begin 2018.

Bailey Falter is another 20-year-old lefty that had a very good season in 2017 for Lakewood. He went 8-7 with a 2.99 ERA in 117 IP with 105 K's and just 23 walks in 21 starts. Bailey throws a bit harder than Fanti but also has the natural lefty tail on his fastball. With all the other young talent in the system he's seemingly overlooked but don't discount this young hurler, he's got really good stuff and also should be in line for the Clearwater staff next spring.

Andonis Medina is yet another 20-year-old who pitched very well for Lakewood this past year, he's a right hander though. In 119 IP he posted a 3.01 ERA with 133 K's and just 39 walks. Medina is a power pitcher with a fastball that sits 93-95 with capability of even more. He's got a very good feel for pitching and when he's on, he's a guy that dominates hitters. He too is deserving of a bump up next spring to at the least Clearwater.

Twenty-one-year-old Alejandro Requena came over from the Rockies in the Pat Neshek trade. He went 9-4 in 21 starts with a 2.74 ERA in 128 IP, and he's another exciting young arm with a big upside who should push for a rotation spot in Clearwater.

There's plenty of solid starting pitching also on the short Season squads from 2017 that are ready to bump up to full season rosters for 2018.

Kyle Young had an outstanding year for short season Williamsport. The 19-year-old lefty was 7-2 with a 2.77 ERA in 65 IP with 72 K's and just 15 walks. He's definitely slated for the Lakewood rotation next spring, in my humble opinion this young fella is going to be a star - big time talent.

Four other starters from the 2017 Crosscutters are likely to move up to full season play in 2018. Julian Garcia posted a 3.90 ERA in 13 starts (60 IP) with 82 K's, and he's at least slated for Lakewood I would think, although a move to the bullpen may be the role next year. Ramon Rosso is a 21-year-old right hander who's got a big arm and pitched at all three short season spots in 2017, where sparkled with a 7-1 record and a 1.31 ERA in 75 IP with 105 K's in 15 games with 14 starts. He's definitely going to get a shot at the Lakewood rotation this coming spring. 2017 second round pick Spencer Howard saw limited action in 2017 but the 21-year-old should move up to full season play this spring, likely with Lakewood. Connor Seabold also saw limited action in 2017 but the third round pick from the 2017 Draft is slated to move to full season play this spring.

Twenty-year-old Will Stewart is another young lefty that is slated to move up next spring, he went 4-2 with a 4.18 ERA in 13 games in 60 IP. 19-year-old Andrew Brown made 10 starts at Williamsport but could repeat there if he doesn't move to full season play next spring. Brown posted a 3.11 ERA in 63 IP with 47 K's.

The GCL staff also had talented starters in 2017, although it consisted of mostly teenagers who would seem destined to repeat short season play in 2018, either back in the GCL or at Williamsport. Francisco Morales, Jhordany Mezquita, Manuel Silva, Jose Jimenez and Ethan Lindow are all teenage hurlers who formed the starting staff. They should continue to battle for innings in 2018 spring training, but I'd expect them to all be back in XST next year and also on short season rotations for 2018 play. Ben Brown is another young teenage hurler to watch who's also likely to move into a short season starting role next year. Jakob Hernandez is a 21-year-old lefty who threw exclusively as a reliever this year in the GCL but I could see him being given a long look next spring as a starter with a shot at full season Lakewood.

Leonel Aponte, Jose Conopoima and Bryan Alcala are DSL pitchers who could be rotation pieces in the GCL next summer especially if the Phillies decide to go to two squads. 2017 signees Carlos Bettencourt, Victor Vargas and Alfonso Puello are all 16-year-olds who were in the Florida Instructional League and therefore are very likely going to be in XST and on GCL rosters in 2018. All three were impressive in their FIL outings this fall.

A lot of depth in the starting pitching category in the organization and quality. The pipeline is there for the next five years, at the least of advancement of good starting pitching.

Kevin Gowdy had Tommy John surgery during the season and hasn't really gotten on track since being drafted in the 2nd round of the 2016 draft. He's just 20 years old and has plenty of time to bounce back. The young right hander is very talented and hopefully he will be able to get back on the mound soon. It's likely though that he misses all of the 2018 since while rehabbing.

Depth of the Organization - Relief Pitching

Bullpens seemingly change more from year to year than any other part of big league rosters. Perhaps it's the wear and tear of pitching almost every day that reduces relievers effectiveness over time. It's also rare to find relief pitchers who stay with the same clubs throughout their entire careers. Closers and back-end setup pitchers are somewhat more stable than the middle inning relievers but even there there's a good deal of movement. It's one of the least predictable areas of a roster but also one of the most important in today's game with fewer starters going beyond the sixth inning in any regularity, as the major league average for 2017 was 5.51 IP by starters (the Nationals were the best at 6.17, Phillies starters averaged 5.49). In today's game younger pitchers are even developed as relievers with specific roles in mind. Here's a look at the bullpen depth as it stands for the Phillies organization.

The Big Club:

The Phillies ended the season with a relatively stable set of relievers and role definitions. Lefties Adam Morgan and Hoby Milner had excellent second halves, and Mark Leiter, Jr., Edubray Ramos, Luis Garcia and Hector Neris put up solid numbers. Yacksel Rios and Victor Arano, in their brief big league stays, also were impressive. The Phillies have traditionally carried 12 pitchers on the roster each season, so these six guys would seemingly have a leg up on the competition for the seven bullpen slots heading into spring training.

Adam Morgan blossomed in the second half and became a very viable back-of-the-pen option. The 27-year-old lefty posted a 1.69 ERA in his last 21 appearances of the season. His fastball velocity jumped to 95-97 and he established a slider that became a strikeout weapon. Morgan went from being the seldom used long man, perhaps the most difficult spot on the 25-man roster, to a go-to reliever. Many "fans" were using him as the boo bird whipping boy prior to his success in the second half, but Adam shut them down with his second half performance. Can he maintain what he did the last 21 games? I believe he can. The shorter stints of relieving as opposed to long relief and starting seem to suit him both in confidence and command. If the Phillies don't believe in the young man I'm sure plenty of scouts noticed and there will be quite a few trade inquiries this offseason.

Twenty-six-year-old Hoby Milner posted a 2.01 ERA in 37 games (31.1 IP) during his rookie campaign. The sidewinding lefty uses deception and movement to get batters out, as he recorded 22 K's but had too many walks with 16, plus four hit batters. Milner is no fluke - he's had similar success the past couple seasons at Reading and Lehigh Valley (2.60 ERA in 27 IP at Lehigh Valley this year and 2.49 ERA in 65 IP in 2016 at Reading and Lehigh Valley). He doesn't possess the big fastball that Morgan has, as he hovers around 89 MPH with his heater, but the motion, movement and deception make both his fastball and slider effective pitches. At the least he's got a role as a lefty specialist, but he's proven he can be more than that if given the opportunity.

Twenty-two-year-old Victor Arano made his big league debut this summer and was very impressive. The right hander was 1-0 with a 1.69 ERA in 10 games (10.2 IP) with 13 K's. He's got a nasty slider that has a sharp break but also can bring the heater in the 94-96 range consistently. Victor didn't throw many innings this summer as he was hurt in spring training, placed on the DL in April and not activated till May 30 with elbow issues. His rehab with Coach Burris in Clearwater went well and he pitched himself onto the big league roster via a September call-up. If the young man from Mexico can stay healthy he's got a definite shot at sticking in the Show this coming spring. Ruben made a pretty good deal with the Dodgers on August 28, 2014, getting Arano and Jesmuel Valentin for Roberto Hernandez.

Thirty-year-old Luis Garcia has always had big league talent, as he's got a fastball that sits 97-98 and a wipeout slider to go with it. The only thing that has held him back is himself. Luis's lack of confidence has been evidenced by lengthy amounts of time between pitches, where at times he was like a human rain delay. Something clicked for him in the second half of last season though and not only did he pitch with tempo but also conviction. In his last 46 appearances of the season he posted a 2.03 ERA, and was even better in his last 23 games when he had a 1.61 ERA. At times he was truly dominant, and he pitched like his talent should play. If Luis can come back this spring with the same confidence and approach, then the eighth inning is well taken care of.

Mark Leiter, Jr. has pitched in various roles his entire minor league career, doing whatever is asked of him. His rookie season in the Show was no different as he pitched both as a starter and a reliever. He was used in long relief initially but his moxy, talent and makeup moved him into more prominent roles. He ended up throwing 90 big league innings in 27 games, 11 as a starter. The 26-year-old throws six different pitches, including a four-seam fastball that hovers around 91 MPH. He's a manager's delight as he is so versatile. Mark should strongly compete for a staff role again this spring.

Twenty-eight-year-old Hector Neris took over the closer's assignment this season. He ended up with 26 saves in 29 chances and posted a 3.01 ERA in 74 games (74.2 IP) with 86 K's. Hector features a splitter that drops straight down when he stays on top of the release point, but also has the ability to bring the heater in the mid 90's. He went 20-for-20 in save chances after June 28 and posted a 1.37 ERA in those games. He's had two solid seasons the past two years and has earned the opportunity to be the closer going into next season.

Twenty-three-year-old Ricardo Pinto was shifted to the bullpen after struggling in eight starts to begin the season with Lehigh Valley. He's got a live arm with a fastball that sits at 94-95 but lacks movement. The straightness of the pitch made it very susceptible to big league hitters and he struggled in 29 IP posting a 7.89 ERA. Ricardo needs to work on other pitches along with gaining more movement on his heater, he has a four-pitch repertoire, including a sinker. 2018 is likely a year he spends time at Lehigh Valley doing just that and with success he could be back in the show.

Twenty-four-year-old Edubray Ramos suffered through a lack of self-confidence early in the 2017 season and it resulted in a demotion to AAA Lehigh Valley. He's got a big arm with a mid-90s fast ball and a Luis Garcia-like slider, and also possesses a splitter that's comparable to Neris'. After his stint in Lehigh Valley he came back to the big leagues and performed very well. Ramos posted a 0.93 ERA in his last 16 appearances. He should be in line for a 2018 bullpen slot going into spring training.

Yacksel Rios received the call to the Show on August 22 and appeared in 13 big league games (16.1 IP) accumulating 17 K's and posting a 4.41 ERA. The 24-year-old from Puerto Rico has a fastball that sits 94-95 and features a hard slider and straight change. He had a great minor league season posting a 1.92 ERA in 37 games (56.1 IP) between Reading and Lehigh Valley. He also recorded an outstanding WHIP of 0.82. Yacksel showed that he has the stuff to be a big leaguer, and this spring he will get the opportunity to prove that he belongs there long term.

Twenty-four-year-old Jesen Therrien also earned a big league promotion this summer after a stellar minor league season in which he posted a 1.41 ERA in 39 games (57.1 IP) between Reading and Lehigh Valley. He had a WHIP of 0.84 using a devastating slider and mid 90s fastball to dominate minor league hitters. Unfortunately, Phillies big league fans didn't get to see him at his best as he suffered a season-ending arm injury which required Tommy John surgery. It was evident Jessen wasn't the same pitcher when he came to the big leagues as the slider didn't have the bite nor the fastball the velocity he had shown in the minors. It's likely a lost season to rehab for Jesen in 2018 with the hopes he can recover to compete again in 2019. Jesen was outrighted off the 40-man roster and subsequently signed a free agent contract with the Dodgers.

Zac Curtis, Alberto Tirado and Mark Appel are all on the verge of breaking out. Curtis, a 25-year-old lefty, was claimed off waivers from the Mariners in mid-September and appeared in three games with the Phillies. He's a situational pitcher whose fastball sits around 90 MPH. Appel spent most of the summer on the DL with a right shoulder strain, and the intent is now to convert the 26-year-old to a full time reliever, as he's assigned to the Lehigh Valley roster once again. Tirado is just 22 but has yet to resolve his command issues. He's got a big arm with an upper 90s fastball but continued to struggle to throw strikes in 2017. He's also been converted to a full time reliever now.

The Minor Leagues:

At the end of the season Lehigh Valley's bullpen consisted of veteran pitchers that seemingly don't figure to be major league contributors. Michael Mariot, Pat Venditte, Pedro Beato, Cesar Ramos, Colton Murray and Mark Peterson all finished the year with the IronPigs and all are likely to move on this offseason, although a few could be re-signed to fill out the Lehigh Velley roster. There's likely to be quite a few minor league free agents signed to fulfill the IronPig's roster this year as the movement of the young talent to Philadelphia has left a void. As of this writing Venditte had signed with the Dodgers and Mariot with the Padres.

Twenty-five-year-old lefty Joey DeNato and 23-year-old righty Alexis Rivero likely return to Lehigh Valley, and both could still develop into major league pitchers. DeNato is somewhat of a clone of Hoby Milner, though not as big physically, and Rivero is similar to Yacksel Rios in repertoire.

The Reading bullpen at season's end had three up-and-coming lefties in Austin Davis, Jeff Singer and Tom Windle.

Davis went 6-2 with a 2.60 ERA in 62.1 combined innings between Reading and Clearwater. The 24-year-old was the club's 12th round draft choice in the 2014 draft out of Cal State Bakersfield. He features a mid-90s fastball and a slider. Austin spent time on the DL in late August with an elbow strain, and he should be a candidate for the AAA bullpen crew this spring. Singer is also 24 years old, and he went 5-4 with a 3.00 ERA in 49 games (63 IP) between Clearwater and Reading, with 21 saves in 23 chances. Jeff also brings the heater in the mid 90s. He comes into spring training with a likely shot at the primary closer role for Reading to begin 2018 but also the possibility of making the Lehigh Valley roster. Windle is 25 years old, and while he's battled command issues most of his career, he has an even bigger arm than Davis and Singer with the ability to hit upper 90s on the radar. He performed better in the second half of the 2017 season after spending some time on a rehab assignment in Clearwater where he was tutored by Roy Halladay. Windle was 1-0 with a 2.86 ERA in the second half in 28 IP with 23 K's. He should get a shot at the Lehigh Valley bullpen this spring.

Garrett Cleavinger is a 23-year-old right hander whom the Phillies acquired in the Jeremy Hellickson trade. He was Baltimore's third round draft choice in the 2015 draft. Cleavinger is representing the Phillies in the Arizona Fall League this year. He's battled command issues thus far in his pro career but has a big arm, and hopes are he can control it.

Shane Watson was converted to the bullpen in 2017 and had mixed success, as he posted a 4-5 record with a 4.10 ERA in 33 games (83.1 IP) and struggled with command walking 40 batters. Miguel Nunez finished the season on the injured list with biceps stiffness after going 1-4 with a 3.47 ERA in 36.1 IP. Nunez is a free agent this offseason.

Ranfi Cassimiro re-signed with the Phillies rather than test free agency. The 25-year-old RHP threw 82.1 innings in 2017 with a 3.39 ERA. He will be a Reading/Lehigh Valley candidate in spring training.

JD Hammer came over to the Phillies organization from the Rockies in the Pat Neshek trade. The 23-year-old was drafted in round 24 in the 2016 draft out of Marshall University. His overall record for the summer was 6-2 with a 1.87 ERA in 57.2 IP with 85 K's and just 16 walks, and he was 2-0 with a 0.57 ERA for Clearwater in 15 IP. Hammer also pitched well in the Arizona Fall League and is considered a very good prospect. He's a hard thrower with a fastball in the mid to upper 90s and a nasty slider to boot. JD should move up to Reading next season.

Luke Leftwich converted to a full-time reliever in 2017. The 23-year-old seventh round draft pick in the 2015 draft from Wofford College struck out 98 batters in 80 IP with a 2.70 ERA in 42 games. He spent the entire season with the Threshers. Leftwich also can bring the heater in the mid 90's and also should be targeted for the Reading club for 2018.

Blake Quinn and Harold Arauz were starters/long men for Clearwater. Both had success but Arauz had a stellar season, which included throwing a seven-inning no-hitter on July 30. He tossed 96 innings at three levels in 96 IP with 93 K's. Quinn struggled as a starter but fared much better as a reliever and posted an ERA of 3.68 in the second half coming out of the bullpen in 19 games. Both should play similar roles next summer with Reading in their sights.

Twenty-three-year-old Tyler Gilbert also switched to the bullpen after being a starter the previous two seasons of his career. The 2015 round six draft pick out of USC is a lefty and posted a 2.95 ERA in 35 games (61 IP). He should also compete for a role on the Reading staff in 2018 spring training.

Seth McGarry came to the Phillies from the Pirates organization in the Joaquin Benoit trade. He was their eighth round pick in the 2015 draft out of Florida Atlantic. McGarry tied with Jeff Singer for the Florida State League saves leadership with 19. He posted a 2.32 ERA in 44 games (54.1 IP).

Trevor Bettencourt had a very good 2017 season, his first full year as a pro, and was assigned to the Arizona Fall League for his efforts. He went 5-2 with a 2.61 ERA in 41 games between Lakewood and Clearwater. He pitched 58.2 innings and recorded 77 strikeouts with just nine walks. He's got a devastating curveball that he uses as his out pitch. Trevor should be in Reading for 2018.

Twenty-four-year-old Will Hibbs had an outstanding season at Lakewood. He went 6-4 with a 1.77 ERA in 40 games posting 20 saves. Will struck out 73 batters in 61 IP for the BlueClaws. He had a brief stint at Clearwater also before finishing up the year back at Lakewood. Will is slated to be at Clearwater for 2018 at the least.

Mauricio Llovera, Ismael Cabrera, Jonathan Hennigan, Casey Brown, Tyler Hallead, Addison Russ and Jake Kelzer each contributed to the Lakewood relief corps this past season and each will be given a shot in spring training to earn advancement to Clearwater for 2018.

Short Season:

There were a few standouts in the pen this past season for the short season clubs. At Williamsport, both Randy Alcantara and Luis Ramirez made the New York-Penn League All-Star team. Alcantara is 21 years old and posted a 2-1 record with a 2.23 ERA in 19 games (44.1 IP) with five saves in five chances and four holds. He struck out 40 batters, featuring command of the strike zone with three pitches, he's got a 2.34 ERA in four minor league seasons with 153 IP with a 10-4 record. Randy should be on a full season roster in 2018, likely with the BlueClaws. He's been consistent his whole career and has somewhat flown under the radar so far, but he's someone we should take notice of who has real talent.

Ramirez is 20 years old and moved up from DSL to Williamsport. In two pro seasons he's recorded 22 saves in 25 chances with a 1.72 ERA in 57.2 IP. Luis has an above-average heater sitting mid 90s and a very good splitter. He's certainly one who will be in full season play next season, likely at Lakewood.

Connor Brogdon, Damon Jones, Zach Warren, David Parkinson and Connor Seabold were all 2017 draftees that pitched out of the Crosscutter bullpen in 2017. Seabold will likely become a starting pitcher in 2018 and each of the other guys will be given opportunities in spring training to move to full season play with both Low-A and High-A levels in their sights.

Anton Kutznesov and Jakob Hernandez were standout relievers for the GCL Phillies. Neither is a "hard thrower" and both rely on command and off-speed pitches to succeed. Kutznesov is 19 years old and hails from Russia, and converted five saves in five chances with a stellar 0.36 ERA in 15 games (25.1 IP) while Hernandez, a 21-year-old lefty, recorded a 1.64 ERA in nine games (11 IP) with 15 k's, he's got a devastating straight overhand curve ball. Jakob should move to full season play next summer.

Denny Martinez, Victor Sobil and Oscar Marcelino are young relievers who pitched for the GCL club this summer and should move up the chain in 2018.

From the DSL rosters we should expect that Ludovico Coveri , Victor Santos, Abdallah Aris, Moises Nolasco, Alfredo Benitez, all relievers who had good seasons in 2017, likely will be considered for promotion to the states for GCL rosters, especially since the Phillies plan to have two GCL clubs in 2018.

Two right handers suffered season ending injuries during spring training in 2017 which required surgery. They spent the summer in rehab. Sutter Mcloughlin recorded 14 saves for Lakewood in 2016 even with a sore shoulder, he got it surgically corrected this past spring and looks to make an even stronger impression once he's fully healthy. The 6'6" twenty four year old has a power arm and is a back end of the pen guy. Look for him to get back on track in 2018. Grant Dyer was the team's 8th round draft pick in the 2016 draft and had a very good initial season posting a 2.34 ERA in 42 1/3 innings between Williamsport and Lakewood. Dyer features both a devastating curve and slider and is the ultimate strike thrower, he had only 6 walks with 57 k's his first pro season. Grant underwent arm surgery and missed all of the 2017 season, once he's mended the 22 year old should be solidly back in the mix as a bullpen prospect.

Alex Kline also missed the entire 2017 season, he suffered a back injury during spring training. Alex is a power arm left-hander

Chapter Fourteen - In Memoriam - Those We Lost

The Phillies organization grieved the deaths of some great folks in 2017. These men all had huge impacts on the organization and will be sorely missed. Here's my memories of three of the gentlemen we lost. These tributes were written at the time of their passing.

March 23: Mr. Green

As all Phillies fans now know, Dallas Green passed away yesterday. The news hit the Phillies hard, particularly those who have been around awhile, which is quite a few folks. Like their baseball decisions and approach or not the Phillies treat those within the organization as family and deaths of family are the most difficult to deal with. Pete Orr, who is presently a scout with the Brewers, told me the other day that the reason coaches and personnel stay with the Phillies so long is because they treat people right and they want to stay because of that, little things like acknowledging the birth of children, helping out in times of illness or strife and providing encouraging words and even kicks in the tail when needed. These are all things families do for one another.

From what I gather, it's a description of how Mr. Green lived his life as well. As fans we saw the public part of how he led the 1980 crew to a championship by challenging them as they had never been "encouraged" before. We also saw a grief-stricken Mr. Green when he lost his granddaughter tragically that horrible day in Arizona. We saw a person who loved baseball with passion and served our Phillies with equal desire and dedication. We saw what we believe ourselves to be as fans in Mr. Green.

I call him Mr. Green out of respect, always have. I had the good fortune to shake his hand on a couple occasions at the Complex. He usually was up above on the upper level walkways and field overhangs with his big-brimmed hat on, observing the practices and games just like I and many others do from the ground and bleachers. Mr. Green could be heard from those bleachers when he spoke to whomever from that overhang, his voice and appearance left no doubt as to whom he was. Often I would overhear fellow fans state "that's Dallas Green." The respect folks had for him was evident, and the stories I have heard folks tell about him in my various conversations at the Complex have always reflected that reverence.

As a Phillies fan I feel saddened by his death. It's always disheartening when someone passes from this life. My condolences go out to my fellow fans but primarily to Mr. Green's relatives which very much includes the Phillies, it's just how they are, a family. There will be remorse in camp today for a family member has passed. Rest in Peace Mr. Green, you will never be forgotten but you surely will be missed.

Darren Daulton passed away on August 6, my mom had passed away on August 4. I wrote this letter to the Phillies when I heard of Darren's death.

I think the tribute you folks are doing tonight is really cool and is a great testament to Darren. I thought I would share my own interaction with him from a fan's perspective. As you may know I also have a brain tumor (mine is benign and is stable), I completed radiation treatments about four years ago.

After my treatments four years ago I attended Phantasy Camp and the "wish" I listed on my request card was to meet Darren Daulton. I wanted to tell him that I was a fellow tumor survivor, he had just completed his surgery and was in the midst of radiation at that time. My team "legend" Marty Bystrom arranged for my wife and I to meet him at the banquet. I wanted to encourage Dutch that everything was going to be OK but he actually was the one who encouraged me more, made me feel secure that I could overcome and that I had a long life ahead of me. I was really struck with how much he seemed to care about me, we had never met, and he was going through many more struggles than I as his tumor was cancerous and required surgery, while I merely had radiation treatments. He was extremely though, and I could see why his teammates held him in such high regard. Dutch hugged me and my wife that night as if we were lifelong friends. That was really cool.

This year at Phantasy Camp he was hardly able to walk, Tommy Greene had to help him, and I saw Tommy weep afterwards. Darren was truly loved by those guys, it was so evident.

My mom just passed away this Friday, August 4. I am in mourning for her as we will lay her to rest this coming Friday. Hearing the news about Darren hit hard as well but then I thought how my mom was also such a caregiver and helpful soul. In my mind they arrived in heaven together, Dutch opened the gates for my Mom and she made sure he came along as well. Two people I loved in different ways together entering eternity. I at least find some comfort they are there together.

Roy Halladay tragically passed away in November in a plane crash. He was just 40 years old. We fans perhaps felt his loss the most. We were humbled as fans to be able to share in his life celebration with his family and friends at Spectrum Field a week after his death. Here were my thoughts after I found out about his passing.

When you're a sports fan, the players who represent your chosen team often become bigger-than-life in your eyes. The games in which they participate, especially the ones where they excel, become embedded in your memory. If they win a championship or get your team into the playoffs they become legendary, especially if your team doesn't usually win all that many games.

As Phillies baseball fans we've suffered more than our fair share of losses and the accompanying heartache. We're known collectively as demanding and critical but also as loyal and passionate. When a player wears our colors, he becomes ingrained in our desire to succeed and we especially endear those who have great work ethic, passion and desire to win. These men become our heroes and are revered. We hold them in awe and high esteem.

Roy Halladay held such reverence in Philadelphia amongst us fans. He wanted to play here, wanted to win more than anything and worked harder than anyone to produce a championship. He was also a man of compassion and served the community via charitable actions, mostly unpublicized, through various off-field endeavors.

I just saw him a few weeks ago in Clearwater at the Complex during Florida Instructional League play. He was up on the observation deck watching the game that day. I never had the pleasure of talking with him, never got to know him, but as a fan felt like I did anyways.

This past year or so he was a regular at the Complex working with the minor league players in spring training, extended spring and with those on rehab. I've read many of their testimonials to Roy the past couple hours on Twitter in how they were honored to be mentored by him on the skill of positive thought. That was primarily his role, he was a disciple of mental toughness and envisioning success to make it happen. He used it himself to reinvent his career after early failure.

Roy coached his sons and their teams in baseball as well, just recently he had posted on Twitter a 12-and-under tournament championship and how proud he was of the kids. He coached at a local high school and they also won a championship. He loved to fly and posted Twitter items on that as well. Recently he had gotten a new plane, the first of its kind from what I gather, and he was very proud of it and the experiences it gave him. He posted multiple pictures and even a video of how the views were breathtaking. From what I could gather he took the plane up at every chance he got, he even stated his wife didn't want him to get the plane but he convinced her it was "all good" and that even she was enjoying the flight experiences. He seemed really excited and happy when flying from the posts he recorded.

Today we were at Spectrum Field watching the Men's Senior Baseball League tournament play when I got a text from a friend quoting a local tv report that Halladay's plane had crashed. We found out later he had died in the crash. Even though I never truly knew him my heart sank, no doubt every Phillies fan heart did the same. I wasn't going to write anything about it as I really have no words to express my sincere grief for Roy's family, especially his wife and two boys. I can't imagine what they must be going through right now. It's so very sad.

As a sports fan the players become bigger than life in our eyes, when something like this happens it brings home the reality that they are mortals just like us. We grieve the reality of their loss, it's disheartening and sudden and oh so sad. It's part of the cycle of all our lives that's inevitable but we are never truly ready for. Time will help heal our sadness, our memories help us cope. We fans feel the loss almost as if it's our own family. In our minds and hearts it is.

To the Halladay Family my sincere and heartfelt condolences, and to the Phillies organization as well. To my fellow Phillies fans, I too feel your sadness and loss, we are indeed all family and we've lost one of our best. Together we grieve. Thank you, Roy, for what you gave us, May you Rest In Peace, that ball team skipper in Heaven just brought home another ace.

The team lost two others during 2017 as Jim Bunning and Ruben Amaro, Sr. each passed away as well.

May Dallas, Darren, Ruben, Jim and Roy Rest in Peace. They all are surely missed. I know my Mom Hazel is up in heaven with them making sure they are still playing baseball!

Chapter Fifteen - Team Outlook:

The Phillies hired Gabe Kapler from the LA Dodgers as the new manager in October after moving 2017 skipper Pete Mackanin to a front office advisory position. Kapler brings a progressive outlook to the club emphasizing analytics and health care year-round. He's a younger manager at age 42 and is tasked with communicating to his young team that they are very capable of winning. There's talent for sure, it's just a matter of whether they put it together into a winning and cohesive unit.

The initial 40-man roster was set on November 20 and five new young players were added, including Jose Taveras, Ranger Suarez, Seranthony Dominguez and Franklyn Kilome. The 40-man roster at that point consisted of 35 players who had been developed by the Phillies minor league system at some point in their career. It's a true testament to the development staff, scouts and draft team and openly reflects the ongoing happenings of the organization as it works towards sustaining a winning crew at the big league level.

2017 was a true year of transition for the Phillies minor league organization as 14 upper-level players made their major league debut, and others beneath them advanced to fill their shoes at the levels they vacated. There's very good depth and top-level talent in the Phillies system, and the future's bright. The transition continues. It's a good thing, it's all part of it!

Ben Pelletier, Cord Sandberg, myself, Darick Hall and Jim Peyton. The best part of writing this digest is getting to know the people.